"Deb Dana brilliantly crafts accessible and poignantly effective practices of self-exploration that functionally give our nervous systems permission to feel safe and to experience the profound and beneficial integrative processes that spontaneously emerge."

—**Stephen W. Porges,** PhD, creator of Polyvagal Theory, Distinguished University Scientist, Kinsey Institute Indiana University

"In this welcome new book, Deb Dana brings to the public the simple yet profound healing methods she has derived and elegantly adapted from Stephen Porges's paradigm-changing Polyvagal Theory. Highly recommended for anyone wanting to understand, befriend, and learn to regulate their nervous system and thereby find inner peace."

—**Gabor Maté,** MD, author of *The Myth of Normal: Trauma, Illness and Healing in a Toxic Culture*

POLYVAGAL PRACTICES

POLYVAGAL PRACTICES

ANCHORING THE SELF IN SAFETY

DEB DANA

Norton Professional Books

An Imprint of W. W. Norton & Company
Celebrating a Century of Independent Publishing

This book is intended as a general information resource for profession-
als practicing in the field of psychotherapy and mental health. It is not
a substitute for appropriate training or clinical supervision. Standards
of clinical practice and protocol vary in different practice settings and
change over time. No technique or recommendation is guaranteed to
be safe or effective in all circumstances, and neither the publisher nor
the author(s) can guarantee the complete accuracy, efficacy, or appro-
priateness of any particular recommendation in every respect or in all
settings or circumstances.

    Any URLs displayed in this book link or refer to websites that
existed as of press time. The publisher is not responsible for, and
should not be deemed to endorse or recommend, any website other
than its own or any content that it did not create. The author, also, is
not responsible for any third-party material.

For information about permission to reproduce selections from
this book, write to Permissions, W. W. Norton & Company, Inc.,
500 Fifth Avenue, New York, NY 10110

For information about special discounts for bulk purchases,
please contact W. W. Norton Special Sales at
specialsales@wwnorton.com or 800-233-4830

Manufacturing by Versa Press
Book design by Daniel Lagin
Production manager: Gwen Cullen

ISBN: 978-1-324-05227-2 (pbk)

W. W. Norton & Company, Inc., 500 Fifth Avenue, New York, NY 10110
www.wwnorton.com

W. W. Norton & Company Ltd., 15 Carlisle Street, London W1D 3BS

1 2 3 4 5 6 7 8 9 0

To my family. You are my anchors . . .

CONTENTS

ACKNOWLEDGMENTS

Whenever I write, I'm reminded that community is an essential ingredient in my creative process. More than any other of my other projects, this book feels like a shared effort. *Polyvagal Practices* was inspired by a conversation with my editor, Deborah Malmud, shortly after I came home from the hospital and was only beginning to recognize the repercussions of my medical crisis. Upon reflection it was a crazy idea to write around a schedule of twice-a-day home IV infusions, when walking from the bedroom to the kitchen was unthinkable, and I wondered whether I would ever teach again. In the end writing this book was an essential part of my recovery. Putting the pieces of the book together helped me rediscover my purpose and reconnect with my passion for this work. Thank you, Deborah, for reaching out with a lifeline in a time when I felt lost. Much love to my wise and wonderful daughters. Your love and care helped me find the way forward and create the new routines that nourish my nervous system. Without you patiently and persistently reminding me there is another way to move through the day,

I would not be on this new path to well-being. Special thanks to the people in my polyvagal family who were there when I worried that I would never return to some sort of normal. You reminded me I was not alone, reassured me I would be ok, and helped me find a balance between rest and writing. To all the people who emailed me about their experiences with different practices, your stories were important in helping me choose the practices to include in this book. Through emails, Zoom meetings, phone calls, and visits so many people played a part in bringing this book into being. Thanks to each of you for helping me turn toward my growing edges and learn in a deeper way how to anchor myself in safety.

Sending gratitude and a glimmer,

Deb

POLYVAGAL PRACTICES

INTRODUCTION

Polyvagal Practices: Anchoring the Self in Safety is an invitation to learn the ways the autonomic nervous system is both creator of, and witness to, your lived experience. As you befriend your nervous system with the strategies and exercises in this book, you'll discover patterns to celebrate and patterns to change. You will find your way to the rhythm of regulation that brings you safety, connection, and joy. This book was written at a time when my personal life was turned upside down with a medical crisis and the world was in turmoil. Months later, I am recovering and around the globe people are reaching for ways to feel safe while trying to navigate a world that is deeply divided. These unprecedented times are leading us on an individual and collective search to create a safe path forward. Understanding our biology and knowing how to come into autonomic regulation is vital if we are going to safely navigate the challenges of this time of change.

Polyvagal Practices is based on the work of Stephen Porges, the creator of Polyvagal Theory. He first outlined his theory in his Presidential Address at the annual meeting of the Society for Psychophysiological Research in 1994. His address was then published in the society's journal, *Psychophysiology* (Porges, 1995[*]). He has continued to elaborate and expand the theory in articles, books, and lectures. Since its introduction, Polyvagal Theory has been referenced in thousands of peer-reviewed research articles and has been incorporated into the clinical work of therapists around the world. Stephen Porges's development of Polyvagal Theory offers a way to understand the neurophysiological systems that guide our daily living and has greatly influenced the practice of psychotherapy.

Over the years, I have had the joy of collaborating with Stephen Porges to translate Polyvagal Theory first into clinical application and then beyond therapy into everyday use. Polyvagal Practices is written for anyone wanting to build and strengthen connections to the biological state of safety and connection. The book begins with a brief introduction to Polyvagal Theory, followed by practices divided into sections: mapping, listening, connecting, creating, deepening, and reflecting. The introduction will help you become familiar with the basic terms that are used throughout the book and the first two ladder maps in the mapping section give you a foundation for the rest of the practices. Once you have finished those, go ahead and explore the practices in any order you want. Let your nervous system be your guide. Some of the practices have worksheets associated with them. You can find the worksheets at https://www.rhythmofregulation.com/worksheetspvpractices and

---

[*] Porges, S. W. (1995). Orienting in a defensive world: mammalian modifications of our evolutionary heritage. A Polyvagal Theory. *Psychophysiology, 32*(4), 301–318. https://doi.org/10.1111/j.1469-8986.1995.tb01213.x

the meditations within the book are also available in audio form at rhythmofregulation.com.

■ THE SCIENCE OF SAFETY ■

As we prepare to embark on the journey of learning to anchor in safety, it's helpful to understand the basics of Polyvagal Theory and begin to speak the language of the nervous system. We don't need to be scientists—we just need to be curious about how biology shapes our lives and how we can use that knowledge to find our personal pathways to well-being.

You probably learned about the autonomic nervous system in school. Maybe you remember that it controls bodily functions that aren't conscious, such as your breathing, heartbeat, and digestion. That's true, it does. But you might be surprised to learn that it not only controls these vital body functions but is also at the heart of our daily experience. It influences the way we live, love, and work; it guides how we move through the world. According to Polyvagal Theory, the autonomic nervous system operates on three organizing principles: hierarchy, neuroception, and co-regulation.

Hierarchy

The autonomic nervous system is built with three basic pathways of response—ventral, sympathetic, and dorsal—that we move between in a predictable order called the autonomic hierarchy. Each pathway brings its own set of thoughts, feelings, behaviors, and bodily experiences. Ventral, at the top of the autonomic hierarchy, is the system of connection. The ventral state is essential for health and well-being. In this state, we feel grounded, organized, and ready to meet the day. Life feels manageable; we see options, have hope, and hear new stories. We connect to ourselves, to others, to the world around us, and to Spirit. We are regulated and ready to engage. Sympathetic, down one step on the hierarchy, is a system of mobilization. In its everyday function, it helps regulate heart and breath rhythms and brings us energy to move through the day. In its survival role, it activates pathways of fight and flight and pulls us into anxiety and anger. Dorsal, at the bottom of the hierarchy, in its everyday role regulates digestion bringing nutrients to nourish us. When recruited in service of survival, dorsal becomes a system of shutting down. We feel drained, without enough energy to engage with the world. We collapse, disconnect, and disappear. We regularly travel this hierarchy as we navigate the challenges of daily living.

Neuroception

Coined by Polyvagal Theory developer Stephen Porges, neuroception describes how our autonomic nervous system takes in information. This inner, subconscious surveillance system gathers information through three pathways: within our bodies, in the world around us, and in our connections to others. Through neuroception, we are continuously broadcasting and receiving messages of welcome and warning. In response to the information that we receive via neuroception, we move from state to state along the autonomic hierarchy.

Co-regulation

Co-regulation is necessary first to survive and then to thrive. It is a biological imperative—a need that must be met to sustain life. Through reciprocal regulation of our autonomic states, we feel safe to move into connection and create trusting relationships. As we grow, we add the ability to self-regulate, but we never lose the need and the longing to be safely connected to others.

The following beginner's guide offers another look at the autonomic nervous system through the metaphor of the autonomic ladder.

We come into the world wired to connect. With our first breath, we embark on a lifelong quest to feel safe in our bodies, in our environments, and in our relationships with others. The autonomic nervous system is our personal surveillance system, always on guard, asking the question "Is this safe?" Its goal is to protect us by sensing safety and risk, listening moment by moment to what is happening in and around our bodies and in the connections that we have to others. This listening happens below awareness and away from our conscious control. Stephen Porges, understanding that this is not awareness that comes with perception, coined the term neuroception to describe the way our autonomic nervous system scans for cues of safety, danger, and life-threat without involving the thinking parts of our brain. As we humans are meaning-making beings, what begins as the wordless experience of neuroception drives the creation of a story that shapes our daily living.

■ THE AUTONOMIC NERVOUS SYSTEM ■

The autonomic nervous system is made up of two main branches, the sympathetic and the parasympathetic, and responds to signals and sensations via three pathways, each with a characteristic pattern of response. Through each of these pathways, we react *in service of survival*. The sympathetic branch begins in the brainstem and travels the motor pathways that emerge from the middle part of the spinal cord. It represents the pathway that prepares us for action. It responds to cues of danger and triggers the release of adrenaline, which fuels the fight-or-flight response.

In the parasympathetic branch, Polyvagal Theory focuses on two pathways traveling within a nerve called the vagus. Vagus, Latin for wandering, is aptly named. From the brain stem at the base of the skull, the vagus travels in two directions: downward through the lungs, heart, diaphragm, and stomach and upward to connect with nerves in the neck, throat, eyes, and ears. The vagus is divided into two parts: the ventral vagal pathway and the dorsal vagal pathway. The ventral pathway responds to cues of safety and supports feelings of being safely engaged and socially connected. In contrast, the dorsal pathway responds to cues of extreme danger. It takes us out of connection, out of awareness, and into a protective state of collapse. When we feel shut down, numb, or not here, the dorsal vagus has taken control.

Stephen Porges identified a hierarchy of response built into our autonomic nervous system and anchored in the evolutionary development of our species. The origin of the dorsal vagal pathway of the parasympathetic branch and its immobilization response lies with our ancient vertebrate ancestors and is the oldest pathway. The sympathetic branch and its pattern of mobilization was next to develop. The most recent addition, the ventral vagal pathway of the parasympathetic branch brings patterns of social engagement that are unique to mammals.

When we are firmly grounded in our ventral vagal pathway, we feel safe, connected, calm, and social. A sense (neuroception) of danger can pull us out of this state and backwards on the evolutionary timeline into the sympathetic branch. Here we are mobilized to react. Taking action can help us return to the safe and social state. It is when we feel as though we are trapped and can't escape that the dorsal vagal pathway takes us all the way back to our evolutionary beginnings. In this state, we are immobilized. We shut down to survive. From here, it is a long way back to feeling safe and social and a painful path to follow.

▪ THE AUTONOMIC LADDER ▪

Let's translate our basic knowledge of the autonomic nervous system into everyday understanding by imagining the autonomic nervous system as a ladder. How do our experiences change as we move down and back up the ladder?

The Top of the Ladder

What would it feel like to be safe and warm? Arms strong but gentle. Snuggled close, joined by tears and laughter. Free to share, to stay, to leave . . .

Safety and connection are guided by the evolutionarily newest part of the autonomic nervous system. Our social engagement system is active in the ventral vagal pathway of the parasympathetic branch. In this state, our heart rate is regulated and our breath is full. We take in the faces of friends, tune in to conversations, and tune out distracting noises. We see the big picture and connect to the world and the people in it. I might describe myself as happy, active, interested and the world as safe, fun, and peaceful. From this ventral vagal place at the top of the autonomic ladder, I am connected to myself and can reach out to others. Some of the daily living experiences in this state include being organized, following through with plans, taking care of myself, taking time to play, doing things with others, feeling productive at work, and having a general feeling of regulation and a sense of management. Health benefits include a healthy heart, regulated blood pressure, a strong immune system decreasing my vulnerability to illness, good digestion, quality sleep, and an overall sense of well-being.

Moving Down the Ladder

Fear is whispering to me and I feel the power of its message. Move, take action, escape. No one can be trusted. No place is safe . . .

The sympathetic branch of the autonomic nervous system activates when we feel a stirring of unease and a neuroception of danger. We go into action. Fight and flight happen here. In this state, our heart rate speeds up; our

breath is short and shallow. We scan our environment looking for danger—we are on the move. I might describe myself
as anxious or angry and feel the rush of adrenaline that
makes it hard for me to be still. I listen for sounds of danger
and don't hear the sounds of friendly voices. The world may
feel dangerous, chaotic, and unfriendly. From this place
of sympathetic mobilization—a step down the autonomic
ladder and backward on the evolutionary timeline—I may
believe, "The world is a dangerous place and I need to protect
myself from harm." Some of the daily living problems can
be anxiety, panic attacks, anger, inability to focus or follow
through, and distress in relationships. Health consequences
can include heart disease; high blood pressure; high cho-
lesterol; sleep problems; memory impairment; headache;
chronic neck, shoulder, and back tension; and increased
vulnerability to illness.

The Bottom of the Ladder

*I'm far away in a dark and forbidding place. I make no sound. I am
small and silent and barely breathing. Alone, where no one will ever
find me . . .*

Our oldest pathway of response, the dorsal vagal pathway of the parasympathetic branch, is the path of last resort.
When all else fails, when we are trapped and action taking
doesn't work, the dorsal vagus takes us into shutdown, collapse, and dissociation. Here at the very bottom of the autonomic ladder, I am alone with my despair and escape into
not knowing, not feeling, almost a sense of not being. I might
describe myself as hopeless, abandoned, foggy, too tired to
think or act and the world as empty, dead, and dark. From
this earliest place on the evolutionary timeline, where my
mind and body have moved into conservation mode, I may

believe, "I am lost and no one will ever find me." Some of the daily living problems can be dissociation, memory issues, depression, loneliness, and no energy for the tasks of daily life. Health consequences of this state can include chronic fatigue, fibromyalgia, digestive issues, low blood pressure, and respiratory problems.

▪ DOWN AND UP THE LADDER ▪

Now that we have explored each of the places on the autonomic ladder, let's consider how we move down and up. Our preferred place is at the top of the ladder. The ventral vagal state is hopeful and resourceful. We can live, love, and laugh by ourselves and with others. This is not a place where everything is wonderful or a place without problems. But it is a place where we can acknowledge distress, reach out for support, and explore options. We move down the ladder into action when we feel a sense of unease—of impending danger. We hope that our action taking here will give us enough space to take a breath and climb back up the ladder to the place of safety and connection. It is when we fall all the way down to the bottom rungs that the safety and hope at the top of the ladder feel unreachable.

▪ SYSTEMS WORKING TOGETHER ▪

We experience well-being when the three parts of our autonomic nervous system work together. To understand this integration, we leave the imagery of the ladder and imagine instead a home. The dorsal vagal system runs the basic utilities of the home. This system works continuously in the background keeping our basic body systems online and in order. When there is a glitch in the system, we pay attention. When all is running smoothly, the body's functions work automatically. Without the influence of the ventral vagal system, the basic utilities run the empty house, but no one is home. If we are home, the environment is one that brings no comfort. Everything is turned down to the lowest possible setting—enough to keep the air circulating and the pipes from freezing. The environment is just habitable enough to sustain life.

The sympathetic branch can be thought of as the home security system maintaining a range of responses and armed to react to any emergencies. This alarm system is designed to activate an immediate response and then return to standby. Without the oversight of the ventral vagal system, the security system receives a steady stream of emergency notifications and continues to sound the alarm.

The ventral vagal system allows us to soak in, and savor, this home we are inhabiting. We can enjoy it as a place to rest and renew by ourselves and as a place to join with friends and family. We feel the basic utilities running in the background. The rhythms of our heart and breath are regulated. We trust that the monitoring system is on standby. The integration of systems allows us to be compassionate, curious about the world we live in, and emotionally and physically connected to the people around us.

With this initial understanding of the role and responses of the autonomic nervous system in service of our safety and survival, we can begin to befriend our autonomic nervous systems and successfully navigate our quest for safety and connection.

MAPPING

▪ WHY WE MAP ▪

It is difficult to imagine a world without maps. People have been drawing maps for centuries. In 8,000 B.C. Babylon, mapmakers created maps of the sky and stars. The sixth-century Greek philosopher Anaximander is often credited with creating the first map of the known world. Every culture uses some kind of map, and nowadays, many of us don't venture out into the world without a mapping app telling us the best route to our destination.

For sharing the world around us or within us, maps offer the most effective way to simultaneously communicate complex environments and express a sense of place. Their utility for wayfinding . . . is matched by their capacity for inspiring us to explore the world through our imagination . . . [*]

I think wayfinding is a wonderful word. It brings alive the sense of safely traveling from place to place. Wayfinding involves knowing where we are, knowing where we want to go, and having a path to get there. When we create autonomic maps, we become *autonomic wayfinders* using our knowledge

---

[*] The British Cartographic Society. (2016, February). *The Cartographic Journal, 53*(1), 1–2.

of the nervous system to know where we are and safely find our way from state to state.

The goal of autonomic mapping is to illustrate our experience of the world from each state bringing awareness to body responses, beliefs, emotions, and behaviors. When we create an autonomic map, we identify the ways we engage with the world and the patterns of connection and protection that are at work as we navigate our daily lives. We see how our nervous system acts in service of our safety, sometimes responding to an old familiar cue and other times staying grounded in the present moment. Understanding the pathways and patterns of our autonomic responses reduces shame and self-criticism and makes room for curiosity and compassion/self-compassion. Our autonomic maps guide us in choosing practices to find the way back to regulation and strengthen our ability to anchor in safety in the midst of daily challenges.

We use a map when we're lost and need to find our way home. Our embodied home is in the ventral vagal state, safely anchored at the top of the autonomic hierarchy. I believe our nervous system inherently knows the way. We may not have traveled those pathways frequently. They may be partially hidden, or maybe we knew them well once but haven't traveled them recently. No matter our experience, the pathways to safety are wired into our biology and are waiting for us. Our autonomic maps help us orient in the moment and when we know where we are, we can find our way home.

Personal Profile Map Template

The Personal Profile Map is a good place to begin. This map helps you safely connect to, and get to know, your experiences in your two survival states and in the state of regulation. This mapping process invites you to first dip a toe in sympathetic and dorsal survival to begin to get to know those states and not be overwhelmed by them as is often our experience. Then you dive into exploring the energy of ventral safety and connection. While this map can be done in pen or pencil, there is an added benefit to using color. You can use colored markers or pens to fill in the sections. If you don't want to work in color but are curious about the colors your nervous system would choose, consider a color for each state and mark the choice in the margin.

In this mapping exercise, travel the predictable pathway down the hierarchy and first map sympathetic survival, then move to dorsal survival, and finish by mapping the ventral state of regulation. Since our nervous systems respond to mapping our states, we want to end the experience in ventral.

• Remember a time when you were pulled into the sympathetic survival energy of fight and flight, where you felt the rise of anger and anxiety. Let the memory come alive in your mind and body just enough so you feel the flavor of it and aren't flooded by it. Too much and you will be pulled into the chaotic energy of the state and out of the ability to get to know it.

• In the sympathetic section of the ladder map, describe what it is like here. What happens in your body? What do you do? What do you feel? What do you think and say? How is your sleep, relationship with food, and use of substances or compulsive behaviors impacted? As you finish the section, fill in the sentences "I am . . ." and "The world is . . ." These two sentences identify the core beliefs that are driving your experience when you are in a state of sympathetic activation.

• Now move to the dorsal survival state. While in the sympathetic state there is too much energy, the hallmark of the dorsal state is the lack of energy. Remember a time when you felt the energy drain from your system, and you took the first step into shut down. The dorsal experience is one of disconnection, feeling out of touch with the present moment, unseen, lost, and alone. Mapping the dorsal state can easily activate collapse and disconnection. So let just enough in to your awareness that you can be with your dorsal survival state to begin to get to know it.

• Write what it feels like, looks like, and sounds like in this place. What happens in your body? What do you do? What do you feel? What do you think and say? How is your sleep, relationship with food, and use of substances or compulsive behaviors impacted? Fill in the sentences "I am . . . " and "The world is . . . " to discover the core beliefs at work here.

- Finish by mapping the state of ventral regulation. If you're worried that you haven't spent a lot of time in ventral or maybe you think you really don't know that place of safety, you can be reassured that the memory of a micro-moment of ventral is enough to bring the state alive and map it. You don't need long stretches of ventral regulation to become familiar with what it's like there. One moment holds all the information needed to finish your map. You might remember a moment of feeling wonderful, or totally at peace, or joy-filled. You might remember a moment when you felt ok enough, happy enough, organized enough to make your way through the day. All you need is a micro-moment of what I call "ventral OKness." Find a moment, dive in, and bring the state fully alive.

- Write what happens here in this place of ventral regulation. What happens in your body? What do you do? What do you feel? What do you think and say? How is your sleep, relationship with food, and use of substances or compulsive behaviors impacted? Fill in the sentences "I am . . . " and "The world is . . . " and discover the story from this place of regulation.

- While ventral, sympathetic, and dorsal are important terms to know, these names are not necessarily welcoming and how we want to refer to our states. When you've finished mapping, take a moment to connect with each state and then use the boxes along the side of the map to name your states in a way that reflects your personal experience.

Now that you've completed your Personal Profile Map, put it where you can easily refer to it. Check in frequently to find your place on the map. Become a skilled state detector able to easily answer the question, "Where am I?" Notice where you are on your map. Name the state. Turn toward the experience and listen for a moment to what your nervous system wants you to know. "My sympathetic mobilization is telling me . . ." "My dorsal vagal state is letting me know . . ." "My ventral vagal system is inviting me to . . ."

MAPPING YOUR REGULATED SYSTEM

	The world is . . .
Ventral Vagal	
4 Pathways of Connection	I am . . .
	The world is . . .
Sympathetic	
Organized Energy	I am . . .
	The world is . . .
Dorsal Vagal	
Nourishing Nutrients	I am . . .

Regulated Ladder Map Template

In addition to understanding the way our nervous systems use survival energy, we want to get to know the everyday, regulating roles of our three states and what it's like to inhabit a regulated system. The Regulated Ladder Map is a good companion to the Personal Profile Map. Because you are mapping regulated states, you can work in any order you want. I like to travel up the hierarchy from dorsal to sympathetic to ventral, but let your nervous system be your guide.

- Feel the slow and steady beat of your dorsal system. Its regulating role is to bring nutrients to nourish you and offer you a place to rest and renew. Enter into that experience and notice what happens in your body, what you think, feel, and do. Write what you discover on your map. Finish by filling in the same sentences as you did on your Personal Profile Map: "The world is . . ." and "I am . . ."

- Moving up to the sympathetic system, feel the energizing, organized energy of regulated mobilization. In its everyday role, the sympathetic system is responsible for adjusting heart and breath rhythms and bringing you the energy you need to move through the day. Step into the energy of this system and explore the experience. Document what you discover about what happens in your body, what you think, feel, and do in this place. Finish by filling in the sentences: "The world is . . ." and "I am . . ."

- Come to the top of the hierarchy and the place of ventral safety and regulation. Continue the exploration you began when you filled out your Personal Profile Map. Look at the four pathways of connection—to yourself, others, the world, and Spirit—that are engaged and alive in this state. What happens in your body, what do you think, feel, and do? Finish by filling in the sentences: "The world is . . ." and "I am . . ."

Take a moment to look at your completed map. What did you discover? What are the details that are important to you? What do you appreciate about the ways your three states work to bring you well-being?

CREATING ART MAPS

When we create autonomic art maps, we bring the right hemisphere and its love of imagery into action. Because the right hemisphere is less influenced by prediction, what emerges often brings surprising new awareness. You don't have to be an artist to make an art map. You only need materials and a willingness to experiment. There are lots of ways to create an art map: collages on poster board using old magazine pictures, drawings with markers or crayons, painting, or even using objects from nature. Art maps come in all shapes and sizes and are made with many different materials. The experience of art mapping is only limited by your imagination. You might decide to make three maps (one for each state) or one map with all three states represented. Representing one state fosters an intimate connection to that autonomic experience, while illustrating the hierarchy brings awareness to the relationship between states. You can create art maps of survival states and regulated states. Gather your materials, decide on the style of your map, and let your nervous system guide you.

When you finish your map, take time to reflect on what you created. Creating an art map is a personal process. Our maps have their own shapes and stories. See what you put on your map that affirms something you already knew and what might be new information. Give your artwork a title to represent the essence of the autonomic story being told.

Sharing Maps

Remembering that we have a built-in biological need to connect with others, autonomic mapping is an opportunity to invite people around you to create their own maps. Sharing maps is a different way of getting to know each other. While you may know details about someone's life, with an autonomic map you connect in a new way as you learn about each other's states and patterns.

Return, Review, Reflect, Revise

Our autonomic maps reflect an understanding of our system at the time we create them. They are living documents meant to be modified as we get to know our states and patterns more intimately. Art maps capture our relationship with our nervous system in a moment in time. If you are drawn to making art, return to art mapping when you are curious about an experience. Create a series of maps and continue to deepen your understanding of the ways your system works. Our ladder maps are a work in progress that we can regularly update as we learn more about our states and discover new information.

It's helpful to return to our maps and review what is there. Reflect on what you knew when you created the map and what you've learned since. Revise your maps adding anything that feels important.

WHAT LIES BETWEEN: CREATING CONTINUUMS

While we often think in categories and gain useful information from that way of engaging with the world, categorical thinking can also be limiting. When we begin to think along a continuum, we see both ends and can then see what lies between. With this broader way of considering our experience, we move out of all-or-nothing thinking and enter the expansive world of both/and. When we see a moment held in a larger perspective, our stories about ourselves and the world are shaped in a new way.

The basic steps for creating a continuum can be applied to any experience you want to explore.

- Draw a line and mark the two ends. While you may choose to use a horizontal or vertical line, continuums also emerge with curves and corners. Let your nervous system guide you in the shape and style.

- For continuums where there is a moment of change from one state to another, it's important to mark the midpoint.

- Name each end (and the midpoint if you've marked one). Take time with this. Often the words we come up with are not what we first had in mind.

- With the line drawn and ends named, begin to explore the space between. Move slowly along the continuum in small increments, stop to name each place, feel the autonomic experience, and listen to the story.

THE MANY FLAVORS OF VENTRAL

Ventral Continuum

The ventral state is more than a feeling of being happy or calm. It is also feeling passionate, playful, alert, purposeful, curious, joyful, at ease, meditative, or blissful. We can stand up for what we believe in and ask for what we need. The hallmark of a ventral state is the neuroception of safety. As we get to know the ventral state, we discover there are many ways to attend to how we experience safety and connection. When we create a continuum of our ventral state, we see the ways that we move from our first small step into regulation to being filled with the energy of safety and connection.

- Using the steps outlined above, draw your line, label the end where you enter in to the energy of ventral regulation, go to the other end and name your experience of being immersed in that state.

- Then explore the space between. You can use words, different shades of color, images, or even movements to mark the shifts. Notice all the ways the ventral state comes to life for you. Fill your continuum with the many flavors of the ventral state.

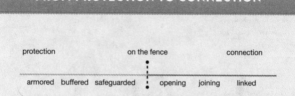

Protection to Connection

We travel the pathway between protection and connection—always somewhere on that continuum. Sometimes we're firmly planted in one place and other times we're pulled from one end to the other. The protection to connection continuum brings awareness to the experience of being safe and engaged or disconnected and in danger. It helps us identify the subtle autonomic shifts that happen as we move between the two experiences. Some points bring a nuanced experience of change while others are where we make a bigger step from one state to another.

- Draw a line (let your nervous system show you the shape). Name the protection end. Name the connection end. Find the midpoint where you feel the change out of protection into the beginning of connection and name that place.

- Travel the pathway from one end to the other naming points, marking the shifts that happen along the way.

- Now that you have created your continuum, stop and see where you are in this moment. You can use the midpoint to first see if you are on the side of protection or closer to the state of connection. Then, identify more precisely where you are on your range of responses. Explore taking one step along the continuum to shape your experience more toward connection. Take a step back toward protection. Get to know the nuances of experience on this pathway.

SOLITUDE TO SOCIAL

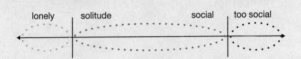

We are social beings who also need times of solitude. When anchored in the ventral state both experiences deepen our ability to anchor in safety. On one end of experience, at the edge of solitude, lies loneliness; on the other end, just beyond safe and social, is the place of overwhelm that comes from a world that is too social. This continuum helps us get to know the ways we are nourished when we are alone and with others, and identify the moment we move from being filled by those experiences to feeling drained.

- Draw your line (let your nervous system show you the shape) and name the social and solitude ends.

- Mark the point where you move from solitude to lonely and name that place.

- Mark the place where you move from social to too social and name that place.

- Move between solitude and social, stopping to mark points along the way. Get to know this part of the continuum. What are the qualities of feeling safe in solitude and in social connection?

- Move from solitude to lonely and notice how you recognize the change. What happens in your body and brain?

- Move from social to too social and notice how you recognize the change. What happens in your body and brain?

- Where are you in this moment? Are you content in this place? Experiment with making small moves along your continuum and see what happens.

TRAVELING FAMILIAR PATHWAYS

We travel the sympathetic pathways of anger and anxiety as our nervous system attempts to keep us safe while managing the challenges of daily life. When we learn to recognize the signs that we are heading into fight-or-flight survival energy, we are better able to change course.

- Get to know the ways your fight and flight pathways come to life. Notice the moments when you feel the building of frustration and anger. Identify what makes you want to fight. Sense the signals from your body. Identify the signals from your mind (your feelings and thoughts). Notice the actions you want to take.

- Notice the moments you feel the building of anxiety and worry. Identify what makes you want to run. Sense the signals from your body. Identify the signals from your mind (your feelings and thoughts). Notice the actions you want to take (physical expression and emotional escape).

As we enter the pathway to the dorsal state, we begin to feel drained physically and emotionally. We feel the disconnected, shut down experience of dorsal in our bodies, thoughts, feelings, and behaviors. Becoming familiar with our dorsal pathway makes it a less mysterious and scary experience. To get to know the ways your dorsal survival response starts to activate, reflect on a moment when you felt yourself moving out of connection into collapse.

- Notice how your body shows you that your energy is draining.
- Listen to the thoughts that emerge. What do you think about yourself, the world, and the people in it?
- Identify the feelings that appear and the actions you want to take.

We have moments, or micro-moments, of being in a ventral state, and by bringing them into awareness, we can turn them into ventral vagal anchors. Ventral anchors are reliable experiences we reach for to help us travel the pathway back to regulation and, once we arrive, stay there awhile. They can be found in the categories of who, what, where, and when, and help us either by reconnecting to the anchor or by activating the memory of the anchor.

- *Who:* Which people in your life make you feel safe and welcome? You might also have a pet who fills that place.
- *What:* What are small actions you take that feel nourishing, regulating, and invite connection? Keep track of the little things that are easy to include in the flow of your day.
- *Where:* Where are the everyday places you move through that bring your ventral state to life? Finding your particular places is important and your autonomic nervous system will guide you if you listen.
- *When:* When are the times you reliably feel regulated?

Keep a list of your anchors and add to it as you discover new ones.

MY HOME AWAY FROM HOME

While we each can be pulled into sympathetic and dorsal survival states, over time we create an autonomic profile and lean more toward one survival strategy than the other. This is our home away from home—the place our nervous system retreats to when the world is overwhelming.

- Notice what happens when you leave the safety of the ventral state. Do you ride out the challenge in the intense survival energy of sympathetic or do you pass through fight and flight and disappear into dorsal disconnection?

- Get to know the ways your home away from home acts in service of your safety. How does it come to your rescue? Consider what might happen if you weren't under the protection of this state.

- Imagine your home away from home is an actual place. It might be a dwelling or a location. Bring it to life in your imagination. Stand at the edge of the environment or on the doorstep of the dwelling and take in the sights and sounds. Enter into your image and get to know this place that protects you.

- Send a message of thanks to the survival state that shelters you when you reach for protection.

COMING HOME TO SAFETY

We all have a home in ventral. Every nervous system is created with a ventral vagal pathway. Our biology includes this wired-in pathway of safety and connection. Stop for a moment and take that in. No matter how challenging our lives are, we can come home to safety.

- What is the feeling of home? Take a moment and see how your nervous system sends you the message you are home. How does your body let you know you are safe?

- What is the picture of home? Imagine a ventral landscape that bring you a sense of safety and invites you in. Take a step into this landscape and explore your home in the land of ventral safety, regulation, and connection. What do you see? Are there elements of the natural world? A house? Animals? People? What are the colors and energy here? What do you smell and hear? Is there a path to walk or a place to rest? Take time to explore. Feel what it is like to inhabit this place.

- What is the story of home? Listen to the story of home that emerges. What are the words that accompany the embodied sense of home and the picture of home you have created?

Tune in to these experiences of home when you feel lost. Trust that your biology knows the way and will help you find your way home.

LISTENING

▪ SAFE ENOUGH TO LISTEN ▪

Most of us don't realize we are part of an ongoing autonomic conversation. Our nervous systems are always communicating with us. While we may talk about intuition
and sometimes act on a gut feeling, we regularly miss the
moment-to-moment information that is moving just below
the surface of awareness. If we don't tune in to the messages
our nervous systems are sending, we don't receive the benefits of the wisdom that is wired into our human biology.
When we do connect with that information pathway and discover there is always something to hear, we can feel overwhelmed. Listening practices help us turn toward the inner
world of our nervous system from an anchor in safety.

When we create a habit of tuning in to the quiet conversations and hear what our nervous system wants us to know,
we can use that autonomic information in making choices
as we move through our day. We are accustomed to listening
to our psychological story but often are not skilled in listening to our embodied story. Our brains say, "we should" or "of
course" to make a quick decision, while our nervous systems
use "maybe" and "what if" to invite a moment of contempla-
tion. Our nervous system is always working in service of our
safety. If we don't slow down and take a moment to listen,

it will find ways to speak louder and louder until it gets our attention. As the nervous system moves to sound the alarm, the more physical and emotional distress we feel. We feel exhausted and in pain, yet we still are unable to listen. We turn away from the messages, disconnect from our embodied state, and shut out the information because somewhere inside it feels too dangerous to hear. We are caught in a story that our brains can only tell in one way and our nervous systems know is unsustainable. When our brains and bodies are not on the same page, our bodies will take whatever action is needed to get us out of the irreconcilable situation. What our nervous system knows and will do to help us survive is quite amazing . . . and undeniable.

■ A DIFFERENT KIND OF LISTENING ■

Hearing is physiological. Listening is a choice. We can listen when we are anchored in the energy of ventral safety and regulation. My dear friend and poet Gary Whited says it so beautifully. "We listen with our ears, yes, but we also listen with our eyes, our minds, our hearts, our touch, and upstream from all sensations and perceptions we listen with our autonomic nervous system."

Neuroception is the way our nervous system listens. Coined by Polyvagal Theory developer Stephen Porges, neuroception describes the way the nervous system searches for cues of safety and watches for signs of danger to help us orient and take action. This internal surveillance system works in the background taking in a constant stream of information and making autonomic adjustments that move us either toward connection or into protection. Neuroception listens through three pathways—inside (what's happening in our bodies), outside (first where we are physically located and then expanding out into the larger world to include neighborhoods, nations, and the global community), and between (both one-on-one and with groups of people). Ordinarily, neuroception is out of our conscious awareness serving our survival and shaping our days. When we bring perception to neuroception, we can travel the three pathways and bring awareness to this otherwise unconscious experience.

NOTICING NEUROCEPTION

Begin to build a practice of noticing the three streams of neuroception.

- The first decision in this practice is how you want to label *safety* and *danger*. These words don't fit for everyone, so the invitation is to find the pair of words that resonate for you (e.g., connect/disconnect, welcome/warn, or approach/avoid).

- Now that you have your words, divide a piece of paper in two and label the sides. Keeping track of the cues is helpful since we often see patterns over time. The cues of danger are often easier for us to recognize, so in this practice we want to make sure to look for both cues of danger and cues of safety.

- Start by looking for one cue of each and build from there. In this moment, can you find one cue of safety and one cue of danger inside your body? From the environment? Between you and another person?

- Stop regularly during your day and do this practice. When you have created several lists, look them over and see what patterns emerge.

After you have worked with this practice for a while, you will begin to see which stream of awareness is easiest for you to connect with and which is hardest. Knowing that, you can lean on the pathway that comes most naturally and give attention to the ones that are less easily available. The inside, outside, and between pathways send a continuous stream of information. When we tune in to neuroception, we listen in new ways and discover the autonomic origins of our stories.

ADDING DISCERNMENT

When signals of danger from the past appear in the present, we can quickly be pulled into survival energy and enter a familiar pattern of protection. What was, at one time, a necessary survival response may no longer be needed. Once we learn to bring perception to neuroception, we can then add context through the lens of discernment. A discernment practice brings awareness to the present moment and supports making an intentional choice rather than simply following an old pathway. Through neuroception we take in a steady stream of information, and cues that have a familiar flavor of danger from our past can pull us quickly into sympathetic or dorsal survival. When a cue from the past reaches into the present, we lose the ability to reflect on our experience as we are taken down an old survival pathway. Discernment helps us notice we are in the present, not the past, in an environment with specific features. If we are around people, it supports our ability to see them and the qualities they bring to the moment. With enough ventral energy alive in our system, we are engaged and curious observers of our experiences.

- It is challenging to do this practice when you are already moving along the survival pathway. To begin, look back on a moment that took you into a survival state and ask yourself the discernment question. *In that moment, with that person or people, in that place, surrounded by those things, was I in danger, or was I safe? Was that intensity of response needed?*

- Once you've gained some skill with discernment through reflection, see if you can bring discernment to a present moment experience. When you feel an intensity of response that seems out of proportion to the actual situation, ask the discernment question to explore your response. *In this moment, with this person or people, in this place, surrounded by these things, am I in danger, or am I safe? Is this intensity of response needed?*

- Sometimes the answer to our discernment question is "yes, there is danger and this level of response is needed." In those times, we can appreciate the way our nervous system serves our safety. Sometimes, the answer is "no." The present moment is in fact safer than our nervous system is sensing, and we can use that awareness to make a different choice.

RECOGNIZING AUTONOMIC INVITATIONS AND WARNINGS

We communicate, one nervous system to another, that it is safe to approach and come into relationship or that it's better to stay away. It is the social engagement system that orchestrates this autonomic experience. The social engagement system came into being in our evolutionary history when the ventral pathway to the heart and four pathways to the face and head formed a connection in the brainstem.

Imagine the social engagement system as your autonomic safety circuit. It is both a sending and receiving system, constantly uploading and downloading information. Each individual element of the social engagement system sends signals either inviting or discouraging connection and at the same time tunes into other social engagement systems looking for signs of warning or welcome.

An ongoing stream of signals is received and sent through the pathways of the social engagement system. The muscle around the eyes (the orbicularis oculi) plays a part in the opening and closing of the eyelid and contributes to the crow's feet that express emotions. This is where the nervous system looks for signs of warmth and an invitation to connect. Our ears tune in to conversations, listening for the sounds of friendship, while our voice broadcasts the meaning underneath our words. Prosody (our tone of voice) is an important nonverbal signal and sends an invitation or warning to another nervous system. Facial expressions convey social information. An unmoving face is seen as sign of danger, while a mobile face is experienced as alive and sending social information. Finally, turning and tilting the head signals availability and interest.

Depending on our past experiences, we may miss or misread the information being received. The following practice helps us attend to the signals being sent between nervous systems. We begin to understand the conversation that is taking place between two nervous systems when we are aware of the cues we are sending and can accurately interpret the cues we are receiving. As we become familiar with this way of listening, we're able to navigate relationships more skillfully.

- Identify the signals being sent from another person that feel welcoming to you. Notice what it is about their eyes, voice, face, and gestures that invites you into connection.

  Their eyes signal safety when . . .

  Their tone of voice sounds welcoming when . . .

  Their face expresses regulation when . . .

  Their gestures convey an invitation when . . .

- Now do the same for signals that send a warning.

- Get to know the ways your own eyes, voice, face, and gestures invite others into connection. Practice sending signs of welcome out into the world.

  My eyes signal safety when . . .

  My tone of voice sounds welcoming when . . .

  My face expresses regulation when . . .

  My gestures convey an invitation when . . .

- Also explore the ways your eyes, voice, face, and gestures send warnings.

SEND AND RECEIVE

It's interesting to see whether the signals we send are being received in the way we intend. Find someone to experiment with and try sending signals along a continuum of subtle to strong. See if what you intend to send is being accurately received. Switch and see if you are accurately receiving what someone else is sending.

CHANGING THE SAFETY/DANGER EQUATION

We can think about our moment-to-moment experience as an equation. On one side are cues of safety and on the other are cues of danger. When the cues of safety outweigh the cues of danger, we are anchored in safety and ready to engage. Sometimes this is a result of the number of cues and other times the intensity of one particular cue outweighs several others. Because the nervous system is always taking in cues, the safety/danger equation is always changing. As the number of cues or strength of cues changes, the equation shifts, and our nervous system responds. Moment to moment, the autonomic nervous system is assessing if there are enough cues of safety to bring us into a readiness for connection or if the cues of danger keep us poised for protection. To tip the balance toward safety, we need to reduce cues of danger and connect with cues of safety.

The signs of safety and danger are sensed through the pathways of neuroception and the social engagement system. This practice can be used to explore in the moment, reflect on a past experience, or to consider an upcoming event.

- Identify cues of safety and danger. Make a list of the cues active in your body, in the environment, and through the pathways of your social engagement system. Mark the ones that are strong enough to counterbalance other cues.

- Review your list and see if the cues of safety outweigh the cues of danger or vice versa.

- If you are content with your equation, take time to appreciate how the variety of cues add up to support your safety.

- If you want to change the equation, look at the cues of danger and see which ones you can reduce or even resolve. Then, see if there are any cues of safety you can bring in or if there are cues already present you can build a stronger connection with.

- As the equation changes so does our story. When you first create the list of cues, stop and listen to the story. Write a sentence or two that captures the theme. Each time you change the equation, take time to write the new story.

AUTONOMIC STORIES

We are living a story that originates in our autonomic state, is sent through autonomic pathways from the body to the brain, and is then translated by the brain into the beliefs that guide our daily experience. The mind narrates what the nervous system knows. Story follows state. We are, by nature, storytellers. We make sense of the world through stories.

- To listen to the beginnings of an autonomic story, take a moment to turn toward your nervous system and tune in for just a moment. Finish these sentences: In this moment, my dorsal state is letting me know . . . My sympathetic energy is telling me . . . My ventral system is inviting me to . . .

This way of listening marks a moment in time, so make a habit of returning to these sentences. Each time you turn inward and tune in, you hear the autonomic plot of your present moment story.

THE STORY OF THREE STATES

As ventral, sympathetic, and dorsal energies ebb and flow, our experience of the world changes. The story that guides our thoughts, feelings, and actions comes from the state that is most active in the moment. At any given time, there are three stories waiting to be heard, one from each autonomic state: dorsal, sympathetic, and ventral.

- To begin to listen to your stories, start with a small, everyday experience that brings a bit of a challenge but doesn't affect your safety or have a significant impact on your life. Look at this experience through the lens of your sympathetic system. What is the story of the experience from that perspective?

- Now consider the experience from the perspective of your dorsal system. What is the story there?

- Once you have heard these two survival stories, come to the regulated state of ventral. Listen to the story being told here in the place of safety.

- Review your three stories and see what you find interesting in each of them. What was expected and what was surprising?

When we listen in this way, we see how each state writes its own story. This is a simple and powerful practice as we notice that nothing in the experience changed, but our relationship to the experience changes through the stories each state tells. When we are pulled into a survival state, it's challenging to remember that there are two other stories waiting to be heard—another survival story and a story of safety. It is often easier to look back on a moment and listen. Even when we are in a place of safety and regulation, it is interesting to remember there are two survival stories in the background and take a moment to listen. This is a good "end of the day" practice. Look back on your day, choose a moment you're curious about, and listen to the stories of your states.

SURVIVAL STORIES

Our survival states come to the rescue when neuroception brings a sense of danger and we feel the need for protection. No matter how irrational the responses may seem, the nervous system is always acting to ensure our survival.

Use the following statements to explore why and how your survival states (dorsal and sympathetic) protect you and appreciate their actions.

- I see that my nervous system is acting in response to ...
- I feel my nervous system protecting me by ...
- My nervous system is working on my behalf by ...
- I am grateful that my survival state ...

When we recognize what is activating our survival systems, become aware of how they are trying to protect us, and appreciate their actions, we can move out of self-criticism and shame into understanding and self-compassion.

HOPES AND WORRIES

Our survival system activates when the safety/danger equation tilts toward danger and we lose our anchor in the ventral state. Sympathetic and dorsal states are effective at protecting us and at the same time also cut us off from people, places, and actions that might support us. The following sentences help you discover the worry of what might happen and the hope of what might be possible.

- Stop when you notice a pull toward sympathetic or dorsal. Identify the worry. Discover what your dorsal or sympathetic state is protecting you from. *If I wasn't (fill in the thought, feeling, or behavior you are experiencing) then (fill in what harm might come to you).*

- Then, identify your hopes and discover what your survival state is keeping you from. *If I wasn't (fill in the same thought, feeling, or behavior) then (fill in what positive experience you could have instead).*

- Return to these questions regularly when you notice you are entering a survival state or as a reflection after you return to regulation. Each experience brings new information.

WRITING AUTONOMIC SHORT STORIES

Our autonomic states begin the creation of a story. Bringing awareness to a moment and adding language connects body and brain so you can hear the emerging story. The following prompts guide you in listening to the elements of your experience to help you write your autonomic short story.

- In this moment my autonomic state is . . .
- My system is responding to . . .
- My body needs to . . .

- I feel . . .
- I want to . . .
- My brain makes up the story that . . .

Use this next prompt to identify familiar patterns and see how your brain creates a story from your embodied experiences.

- When I review my short story, I recognize . . .

Finally reflect on your story and consider how it fits in your present-day life. Is it still a story that represents your experience or is it a story you might be ready to edit?

- When I read my story, I realize . . .

This is a good practice to turn to when you feel a state change and are curious about what's happening. You can also use the prompts to look back on a moment and appreciate where your autonomic nervous system has taken you.

CONNECTING

▪ WIRED FOR CONNECTION ▪

We come into the world wired for connection. From our first breath to our last, we have an enduring need to be safely connected with others. Our autonomic nervous systems never stop needing, and longing for, co-regulation. Within a co-regulated relationship, our quest for safety is realized, and we find sanctuary in the co-created experience of connection. If our experience is that people are dangerous, just hearing that we need connection with others to live a life of well-being can feel scary.

Without reliably regulated people to interact with, the opportunity to create well-being through connection with others is lost. Co-regulating connections bring safety and a sense of belonging. When we are lonely, we lose our sense of place in the world. When our need for connection is unmet, our loneliness activates autonomic responses. Moments of loneliness bring a neuroception of danger activating our survival states. Chronic loneliness sends a persistent message of danger, and our autonomic nervous systems stay locked in survival mode. The consequences of being lonely include depression, anxiety, a weakened immune system, high blood pressure, risk of heart disease, and even premature death. Feeling connected to others is not a luxury; it is fundamental to physical and emotional health.

Co-regulation begins with a shared sense of safety. I feel safe with you, you feel safe with me, and we find our way to connection. This foundation of co-regulation leads to self-regulation. Without experiences of co-regulation and trust that ongoing opportunities for co-regulation are available, the autonomic nervous system remains on guard, self-regulating from a state of survival rather than a state of safety. The good news is that it is never too late to learn to co-regulate.

While connection is a biological imperative, meaning it's something we need to survive, our nervous system has a competing imperative to keep us safe—the drive to survive. Sometimes, these work together. We feel a pull to reach out and find ourselves in a regulated autonomic state that supports connection. Sometimes they work in opposition to each other. We long to reach out but aren't sure our reaching out will be welcomed and a survival state activates stopping us from taking action. Through our physiology, we hear the call to connect and feel an autonomic response. Moment to moment, the autonomic challenge is to balance the drive to survive with the longing to connect.

■ FOUR PATHWAYS OF CONNECTION ■

When we are anchored in autonomic regulation, four pathways of connection are open and available to us: connection to self, others, the world, and spirit. We inhabit our bodies, reach out to others, move through the world with interest, and feel in harmony with spirit. When we are pulled out of regulation, those pathways are disrupted. We lose our sense of self, struggle in relationships, and feel cut off from the world around us and disconnected from Spirit. Finding our way to regulation and traveling the four pathways of connection is challenging. Some days just touching one of the pathways is all we can do and other times we connect to all four with ease. One pathway can seem perennially out of reach, while others may be well traveled. While each of the four connections plays a role in well-being, we create our own combinations of connections and create individual ways to engage with each pathway.

CONNECTING TO SELF

Walt Whitman, in his poem "Song of Myself, 51," wrote, "I am large, I contain multitudes." When we turn toward our inner experience, we find we are all made up of a multitude of parts. Our states offer a home to our parts, and as each state becomes active the parts that are held in that state emerge. We have self-critical parts, parts that blame and shame, parts that see the world as welcoming, and parts that reach out with joy. Often the parts that inhabit each state share common beliefs and act on those beliefs in slightly different ways.

One way to get to know our parts is to create a Parts and Pathways Poster.

- Gather the materials you'd like to use—something to write on and things to write with.

- Move into connection with your internal world and see what parts come to meet you. Returning to your Personal Profile Map to see the thoughts, feelings, behaviors, and beliefs you experience in each state can help you identify the parts that hold these qualities and live

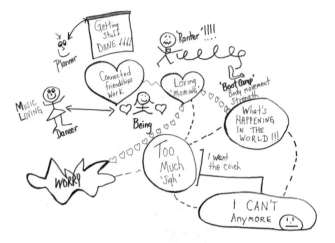

in your ventral, sympathetic, and dorsal states. Parts
commonly found in a ventral state include parts that
are curious, playful, social, organized, ready to connect, relaxed, and move through the world with purpose. In a sympathetic state, we find parts that are
self-critical, self-blaming, workaholic, always looking
for a fight, scared of connection, and anxious. In a dorsal state, we find parts that are hopeless, silent, watching the world from a distance, numb, without energy,
and just going through the motions.

• Decide where you want to place them on your poster. Put
the parts you're most familiar with near the middle and
parts that are less frequently active toward the edges.

• Show how your parts relate to each other through the
distance between them. Draw different kinds of lines
connecting parts (solid, dotted, straight, twisty) to
illustrate the nature of the relationship.

- Name your parts and add words, colors, and images to show how they support connection and act in service of your safety.

Your Parts and Pathways Poster is a work in progress. As you learn more about your inner world return and add more parts and pathways.

▪ CONNECTING WITH OTHERS ▪

While the need for connection with others is universal, the degree of connection and ways we connect are personal. When we make intentional decisions about what we do, how often, and with whom, and find the combination of connections that feels just right, reaching out becomes a regulating resource. A personal connection plan can guide our choices.

CREATE YOUR PERSONAL CONNECTION PLAN

- Name the people in your life you feel connected with.
- Make a list of the things you do with them that brings you joy.
- Think about people you're interested in getting to know and how you would reach out.
- Identify the kinds of things you'd like to explore doing with them.

Use what you have learned to create a combination of what is already in place, what you'd like to try that feels nourishing and resources your connection with others.

Your personal connection plan is a living document. Connections ebb and flow over time. Revisit your plan regularly and update it as things change.

CONNECTING WITH THE WORLD

One of the ways we connect with the world around us is through nature. Connecting with nature is a restorative experience, bringing the autonomic nervous system into a state of ventral safety and regulation. It is a generally accepted that the *green effect* (the impact of being in green spaces) is a powerful contributor to physical and psychological well-being, and that being in a *blue environment* (around or in the water) reduces stress and enhances well-being. Even the simple act of directly connecting to the earth's surface, known as grounding, is an autonomically regulating experience. Seeing the repeating patterns found in waves, clouds, leaves, shells, and blossoms brings a quick return to regulation. The sights, sounds, and scents of nature are regulating and restorative. When we are cut off from the natural world, we feel the disruption.

- Get out into the natural world and look for the places that welcome you. Notice the geography of those places. Get to know the features that are important to you. Visit the places that are regulating for you either in person, through images, or a combination of both.

- Listen for sounds in nature that catch your interest.

- Find your way to water. Being by the water is an autonomically regulating and restorative experience. Look for places around you (ocean, rivers, lakes, ponds, streams, fountains in city parks) that offer the opportunity to be in a blue environment.

- Make a physical connection to the earth's surface. Walk barefoot in the grass, on the ground, or in the sand. Get your hands in the soil or in the sand.

- Bring the outside in. Add flowers and plants to your home and work environments and benefit from their autonomically regulating effects. The smells found in nature are powerful activators of autonomic states. Juniper, lavender, rose oil, and bergamot are some of the scents that have been shown to bring relaxation and regulation. Rosemary, grapefruit, and fennel increase alertness. Discover the fragrances your autonomic nervous system finds renewing and bring them into your everyday experience.

- View nature. Looking out a window at the natural world for as little as five minutes helps you find the way back to regulation after a distressing experience. Images can be used to complement your time in nature or as a stand-in for spending time in nature when opportunities in real time are limited. Find pictures of nature that are autonomically regulating for you and create a collection of them.

- Find fractals. Abundant in the natural world are fractals, simple patterns that repeat over and over creating increasing complexity (e.g., the nautilus shell, a leaf, a pinecone, broccoli buds, dandelions, ice crystals, and clouds). Viewing fractals for just a few moments generates a regulating autonomic response. Look for fractals as you move through your day. Stop for a just a few seconds to take them in. Find images of fractals or objects that have the characteristics of fractals and notice the ones that bring you into a ventral state. An internet search will bring up a wealth of images, and the plants and trees around you offer living examples. Display fractal images or objects in a way that you can easily return to them. (A screen saver, photos on your phone, or a flowering plant or cactus in your home or office are some suggestions.)

We are surrounded by the regulating influences of the natural world as we move through our days. Explore connecting with nature through multiple pathways. Find the particular places and ways to connect with nature that bring your ventral vagal system alive.

CONNECTING WITH SPIRIT

In a ventral state, connecting with something greater than ourselves becomes possible. Connection with Spirit is an intimate, internal experience that expands beyond our individual self and often comes with a feeling of grace. You may feel deeply connected to Spirit, or the experience may feel elusive. Wherever you land along that continuum, when you are filled with the energy of a ventral state, the pathway to connection with Spirit is available.

We connect in many ways including through energy, spiritual beings, spirit animals, and ancestral connections. Invite a connection to Spirit in whatever form it arrives for you in this moment.

- When you say the word "spirit," where does it take you?
- Invite an image of Spirit.
- Listen for a message about, or from, Spirit.
- See if you feel a sense of Spirit moving.
- Write an observation that emerged from this exploration.

Spirit appears in many ways. There is no right way to connect with Spirit—there is only the way of your nervous system. Whether you feel a deep connection or are wondering if you will ever find a connection, keep returning to this exploration and see what emerges.

An understanding of how you connect to each pathway guides your choices about what's needed in the moment. Turn to the pathways that are reliably regulating in the moments you need an anchor and return to the pathways that are less easy to access in the moments when you are regulated and ready to explore.

Reciprocity—the mutual ebb and flow that defines healthy relationships—is a function of the ventral vagus and is an important way the autonomic nervous system stays regulated. Reciprocity is a connection between people that is created in the back-and-forth communication between autonomic nervous systems. It is the experience of heartfelt listening and responding. We feel in our bodies and in our stories the ways caring, and being cared for, bring well-being.

Reciprocity is a way to think about the dynamics of a relationship. Where on the continuum of reciprocal interactions does a relationship fall? We can use an individual interaction to look at reciprocity through measuring qualities of turn taking, talking and listening, the feeling of a "two-way street." But individual moments don't tell the full story of a relationship. Circumstances often disrupt the relational balance. One person has more needs in the moment, and the other shows up bringing regulating energy until there is a return to reciprocity.

In most relationships, the balance temporarily leans, realigns, and leans again. This intermittent inequality naturally deepens the relationship. In other relationships, the flow is more frequently out of balance and a pattern emerges where one person's needs always seem to take precedence. Sometimes, because of accident or illness, the relational balance is permanently changed and the bidirectional flow of reciprocity is replaced by the one-way current of caregiving. No matter the reason, a relationship with a consistent lack of reciprocity feels draining.

OFFERING AND RECEIVING

- Choose a relationship and think about certain moments of connection. Notice the presence or absence of reciprocity.
- Now look at your relationship with that person over time. Is there an ongoing flow of reciprocity that nourishes a sense of connection? Or does the relationship feel consistently out of balance?
- Look at several relationships over time. The ones that have a mutual ebb and flow are resourcing relationships you can depend on.

Remembering a moment of reciprocity engages the capacity of the body and brain to recreate an experience and bring it back to life. A remembered moment inhibits survival states and activates the ventral vagal system and a move toward safety and connection.

- Remember a moment of connection and return to it. Feel the ways your nervous system finds connection in the present as you relive a moment in the past.

▪ PATTERNS AND RHYTHMS ▪

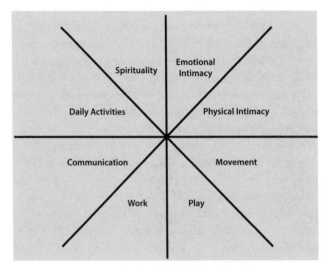

Spirituality

Emotional Intimacy

Daily Activities

Physical Intimacy

Communication

Movement

Work

Play

Looking at autonomic patterns and rhythm brings clarity to places of meeting and missing in relationships—not through narrative but through the lens of the autonomic nervous system. It is a rare relationship that matches in all areas. This leads to the question: Are there enough patterns of connection to feel satisfied, and do the rhythms bring a sense of reciprocity and autonomic intimacy?

We can track patterns of connection within eight broad categories: daily activities, communication, work, play, movement, physical intimacy, emotional intimacy, and spirituality. When we look at the categories of connection, we are checking to see which connections happen and how important each category is for us. Within each of the eight categories, there is a rhythm. When the rhythm brings a sense of meeting, both people in the relationship are nourished.

The rhythm can also bring a sense of missing—coexistence without connection. In an experience of being autonomically out of sync, we suffer.

We can think about daily activities as the ordinary responsibilities of daily living and the ways we take those on by ourselves or share them with another—the division of labor we create with someone and the flow of that during a day. Communication encompasses the many ways we share information including email, text, phone, and face-to-face conversations, the pace of conversations, and the kinds of conversations we have. Work patterns include schedules, time off, and the kinds of work we choose to do; while play includes the ways we play and the times we play. The movement category looks at the concrete ways we navigate through the world and the speed at which we move as we meet the changing demands of a day. Physical intimacy— touching and being touched—includes both sexual touch and the nonsexual friendly touch shared between people and the presence or absence of reciprocity in those experiences. Emotional intimacy is a sense of being in attunement with another person and feeling safe enough to share deep feelings. Finally, spirituality may be religious or nonreligious, practiced in community or individually, and brings a sense of being connected to something larger than one's self.

As we begin to look at a relationship through the lens of autonomic patterns and rhythms, remember that out-of-sync patterns and rhythms don't necessarily mean a relationship can't be nourishing. We each have our own needs for meeting and tolerance for missing. Relationships don't come with a requirement to match in any specific category or move in similar rhythms in order to sustain us.

EXPLORING PATTERNS AND RHYTHMS

- Choose a relationship to explore (partner, friend, family member, coworker).

- Move through the eight categories and identify a general pattern of connection or disconnection for each.

- Review the areas of disconnection. How important is a particular category to you? Are you OK not sharing connection in this way, or is it a relational deal breaker?

- Review the areas of connection and the rhythms within the pattern. Do you and the other person have a rhythm that feels regulating or do you feel out of sync? Questions to consider include: Where are the resourcing rhythms? Is there an out-of-balance rhythm that can be shaped in a new way? Can the areas of imbalance be accepted, and the relationship still feel attuned and in resonance? Are there enough moments of autonomic meeting to sustain overall connection or are the rhythms so dissimilar that reciprocity is unattainable?

- Reflect on what you've identified. Is there enough of a sense of meeting in this relationship to keep you invested in making it work? Are there places of missing that don't overwhelm your ventral state allowing you to accept the mismatch? Are there places that bring an adaptive survival response and need to be resolved for the relationship to feel sustainable?

- With the autonomic story in mind, what are your next steps?

Example of looking at a partner relationship

Daily activities: We have a great "designation of duties" plan. Works well. Things get done and the day feels organized.

Communication: We can have deep conversations, playful ones, and ones about the plan for the day. We don't talk at the same pace, though, and I need to remember to slow down and not get impatient.

Work: Our work schedules are opposite, so there is no match to our patterns. I'm OK with this because we each are passionate about our work, and we have weekends and vacation time together.

Play: We have fun together and enjoy the same amount of play, although we often want to engage in different kinds of play. It works because we each have other people we can call to play in those ways.

Movement: We tend to move at different speeds and are trying to learn to meet in the middle. I find it challenging to find a pace that fits both of our styles.

Physical intimacy: One-sided initiating, not always satisfying. This is an area that is important to me and needs to change.

Emotional intimacy: An on again–off again experience because it still feels very vulnerable and not always safe sharing deep feelings. I have intimacy with other friends but feel the absence in this relationship and want to work on this.

Spirituality: We are similar in our nonreligious, nature-based beliefs, but the amount of spiritual connection we each want doesn't match. I'll participate when asked but I don't often suggest it myself.

Use this practice to look at other relationships and consider the patterns and rhythms each brings. We each have our own needs around reciprocity, and we often find what we need through a combination of relationships.

RUPTURE AND REPAIR

Ruptures are common in any relationship. Moments of missing happen frequently with family, friends, and colleagues and each time we recognize a rupture and make a repair our relationships grow stronger. Our work is to create a habit of noticing the ruptures and a practice of making repairs. Even small ruptures, when unnoticed and unrepaired linger below the surface of awareness and begin to shape the story of a relationship.

There are four steps in the rupture and repair practice: notice, name, normalize, and negotiate reconnection.

• Notice: Ruptures are felt when we experience dorsal disconnection or sympathetic anxiety and confrontation and information from our autonomic state travels to the brain where a story emerges. How does your body send you the message that a rupture has happened? How does your brain communicate that?

• Name: Only when you bring the moment into awareness and name it does it become available for repair and reconnection. When you name your autonomic experience, you have the chance to engage with it, not be caught in it. You may need to take time to first name it for yourself before you are ready to share it, or you may feel ready to name it with the other person as soon you notice and name it yourself.

- Normalize: Through the lens of the nervous system and our survival states, ruptures make sense. You see how biology is acting in service of safety even as it causes a misattunement with someone. When you say to yourself, "That makes sense" then you can begin to have some compassion for where you are, where the other person is, and what is happening.

- Negotiate Coming Back into Connection: Finding the repair that mends the rupture is a process of listening, offering, and staying in the process until there is a sense of reconnection. Sometimes words are what are needed with an acknowledgement of responsibility and a stated intention to change. Sometimes actions bring a repair. You might take an action in the moment or make a plan to do things differently and follow through with it. Reconnecting may happen in a moment, or it may be an ongoing process of working your way back to connection. It's only from the ventral state that you can enter into the repair process. Sometimes you can only notice and name the rupture and need to return to it later when you find our way back to regulation to complete the repair. Sometimes you need to give the other person time to find their way back to enough regulation to consider repair.

The natural and expected cycle of rupture and repair in our relationships forms a foundation for strong and resilient connections. Reconnection after a rupture is sometimes difficult, often painful, and is a practice with which we need to become skillful, because the result is a return to the safety of connection.

CREATING

▪ BEING AN ACTIVE OPERATOR ▪
OF YOUR NERVOUS SYSTEM

The autonomic state shifts we experience in response to the challenges of everyday life are normal and expected. Moving in and out of regulation many times a day is our common human experience. In fact, the goal is not to be permanently anchored in regulation, but rather to recognize when we are pulled out of regulation and find our way back to safety. Our work is to be able to safely navigate the small, ordinary state shifts that a part of everyday life and build the flexibility and resilience needed to weather the changes that are more extreme.

The way we experience daily life is shaped by our nervous systems. Beliefs, behaviors, and body responses emerge from our autonomic states. Physiology and psychology are interconnected. State and story work together. The autonomic nervous system is shaped by our early experiences and is reshaped with ongoing experience. Through the lens of the nervous system, the ways we move toward or away from people, places, and things are understandable and even predictable. When we partner with our autonomic nervous system, we can recruit the power of the system to help us navigate our days differently and write new stories of safety and connection.

Everyday life is filled with challenges. As we move through the day, our autonomic nervous systems quickly respond to assure we survive in moments of danger and thrive in times of safety. With a greater capacity for staying anchored in ventral regulation and the ability to find the way back more easily to regulation from our states of dysregulation, we discover we have an expanded ability to feel safe and connect to the inherent wisdom of the autonomic nervous system. Over time, new skills become sustainable practices. We feel more competent and confident, and we experience the well-being that comes from living with an integrated body–mind system. When we become active operators of our nervous system, we can meet the challenges of daily living with equanimity—we can stand in the middle, anchored in the safety of our ventral state.

STRETCH TO STRESS

Learning to listen to the wisdom of the autonomic nervous system and honoring the right degree of challenge is the foundation for change. The autonomic nervous system doesn't work on the principle of no pain–no gain. Rather than powering through an experience, we want to engage in actions that shape our system in new ways while we are still holding on to our anchor in the ventral state. The process of looking at what stretches and what stresses our system is a way to create just the right degree of challenge to invite in new patterns and deepen ones that are already working.

Imagine the stretch to stress process as two loops and a midpoint line. On the side of safety, we stretch and savor and across the midpoint line we move into stress and then survival.

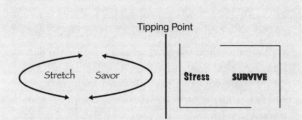

- Draw two loops (use color if you want) and label them with the words you want to use to signify stretch, savor, stress, and survive.

- Add the midpoint line and label that. This is tipping point where you recognize you are moving out of the safety of the ventral state into the energy of survival.

- Choose an experience where you were trying something new or trying to do something familiar in a different way. Track it on your continuum. The goal is to gently shape a new pattern and then spend a moment deepening it. Did you stay on the stretch and savor side, or did you cross over the midpoint into the loop of stress and survive? When that happens, you are no longer shaping a new pattern but instead traveling an old pattern of protection.

- Think about something you want to reshape and use the stretch to stress guide to create a plan to do that. Play with changes that keep you anchored in the stretch and savor loop. See what takes you to your midpoint. Identify what moves you into the stress and survive loop.

Return to your stretch to stress loops whenever you are working with change to track where you are. Honoring your autonomic wisdom is essential in finding the right degree of challenge to support change.

DESIGNING A VENTRAL INSPIRED SPACE

We are nourished in environments that invite connection and inspire an enlivening of ventral energy. When we inhabit spaces that are filled with signs of safety—spaces that invite us to enter and stay awhile—we move toward well-being. Ventral spaces are filled with abundance, but abundance does not mean that the spaces are filled with lots of things. Abundance is felt not in the presence of things but in the presence of our ventral state. Find the balance of open and filled spaces that brings you a ventral feeling of abundance.

- Listen to your autonomic nervous system and become aware of what is present in your environment. Look around the environments you inhabit and notice the places that bring you a sense of regulation and connection and the objects that inspire safety, contentment, and warmth. Identify specifically what it is about those places and things that bring you to this ventral state.

- Look around and see where your sympathetic and dorsal vagal systems begin to activate. What brings those states alive? Notice the places and objects that bring a flavor of unease. Identify their characteristics.

- Make a list of the places and things in your environments that bring a feeling of safety and connection. Identify the specific qualities that feel regulating and resourcing to your nervous system.

- Bring curiosity to what might be possible. Look for a space (a room, a corner, or even a shelf) that could become a place of ventral vagal inspiration for you. Find objects that bring your ventral vagal system alive.

- Make small changes and track your autonomic response to each. Remember, small moments add up to a tipping point. Look for the moment when a space feels welcoming. Stop and take that in.

- Use what you have learned to shape your environments in ways that fill you with ventral energy and bring a sense of comfort.

AUTONOMIC TOUCHSTONES

Touchstones are objects or sensations that have personal meaning, connect us to ventral energy, and help us feel held there. Having touchstones readily accessible reminds us of the predictable presence of ventral energy in our lives and our ability to reach for that connection.

- Find objects that bring you ventral energy and put them in the places you move through during the day.

- Identify smells (one special scent or several different scents) that take you to your ventral state and find ways to bring them into your environment.

- Notice things you wear that reliably help you feel anchored in the ventral state and reach for those on the days you want to feel held in that energy.

Finding touchstones is an ongoing process. Look for new ones. Retire old ones. Move them around your home and work environments. Have ones you can easily take with you or wrap up in when you are heading into a moment that feels challenging.

THREE STATES—THREE THINGS

Finding objects to represent each of the three autonomic states offers a way to characterize our states, understand the qualities of each state in a new way, and explore the relationships between states.

- Choose an object to represent each of your three states. Notice what drew you to each object. Listen to the story each object tells.

- Experiment with different ways to arrange your three objects: lay them side by side; stack them one on top of the other; change the amount of space between them; take the ventral object away, then bring it back. Let your imagination guide you, your nervous system speak to you, and your brain translate the experience into words.

- Keep your three objects where they are easily accessible. When you are feeling regulated, arrange them in a way that represents that experience. When you feel dysregulated, arrange your objects in a way that illustrates your dysregulated state and then rearrange them to represent regulation. Notice how your experience changes. As you rearrange your objects, feel your state shift and story change. Find the way to ventral and anchor there.

NOURISHING SOUNDSCAPES

Sound is one of the strongest activators of neuroception. Our nervous systems are hardwired to respond to sound. Moment to moment, we are searching for sounds of safety.

The many sounds that fill the environment around us create a *soundscape*. Our soundscapes are, in turn, filled with sounds called soundmarks—sounds that are unique to that location and that we associate with that specific soundscape.

- Tune in to your soundscape. Listen to the sound closest to you. Listen to the furthest sound you can hear. Listen in the space between. Where on your autonomic map does your soundscape take you?

- As you move through your day, notice the ways your nervous system responds to different soundscapes.

- Pay special attention to the soundmarks in your soundscapes. Identify ones that activate a survival response and ones that enliven your ventral state.

- Take what you've learned about sound and your nervous system and shape your soundscape in the direction of safety. Look for ways to reduce your exposure to sounds that are dysregulating and actively experience sounds that are regulating.

THE MUSIC OF OUR STATES

Music is all around us, affecting our physiology and our feelings. Along with activating a ventral vagal response, music has a paradoxical effect that allows us to safely connect to, and even enjoy, our sympathetic and dorsal vagal states. With music we can deepen our connection with the ventral state and safely touch the suffering held in sympathetic and dorsal moments that otherwise could overwhelm us. Music is a gentle and accessible way to travel the autonomic hierarchy.

- Create different kinds of playlists. Build collections of songs that take you into safe connection with your three states. For your ventral playlist, choose songs that bring alive the full range of ventral responses (i.e., calm, excitement, passion, compassion, connection, interest, celebration, joy, rest, and restoration). Create playlists that bring a musical revisiting of dysregulated moments as you move into connection with your sympathetic and dorsal survival states. Find songs that represent all the flavors of anxiety, anger, collapse, and disconnection you feel.

- Select songs from each playlist and arrange them in an order that intersperses songs of safety among songs of survival. This listening experience brings a steady flow of moving in and out of states reminding you that you have a flexible nervous system capable of anchoring in safety.

- Reach for your playlists to explore and enjoy your states. Listen with others and experience the joy of shared listening.

REMEMBERING SAFETY

This practice uses sounds, smells, energy, image, and story to remember and deepen into a moment of connection.

- Revisit a moment of ventral connection. Use image, color, sound, smell, energy, and any other elements to bring it alive. Listen to the story that accompanies the moment.

- Now, make a small change. Change one thing that deepens your experience of safety and connection. What is the story now? Take a moment to listen.

- Keep making small changes and listening to the new story until you feel content with where your body and brain have taken you.

BREATHING INTO SAFETY

Autonomic regulation and a story of safety happen when the heart and the breath are in harmony. This synchronization is a function of the vagal pathways. While breath is an autonomic process that works without need for conscious attention, breath can also be consciously shaped.

We typically breathe 18 breaths per minute, 25,902 breaths a day, 9,460,800 breaths a year, and by age 80 will have taken about 756,864,000 breaths in a lifetime. In each of those breaths, there is an opportunity to shape the nervous system toward safety and connection.

Breathing is automatic; we breathe without thinking. We can also breathe with intention, shaping the state of our nervous system. By simply bringing attention to the breath, respiration rate often slows, and breath deepens. The action of placing our hands on our chest, belly, or sides of the ribs brings a physical reminder of the breath cycle and often changes the respiration rate and rhythm. Be gentle when you explore breath practices. Your nervous system has created a way of breathing that has served your survival. When we change our breathing, we change our state.

There are many ways of breathing. Sometimes breath comes in a quiet and rhythmic cycle and other times it arrives in an erratic and stressed way. Different rhythms of breathing change our physiology, making breath a direct route to shaping autonomic responses.

• Use the autonomic hierarchy to map the many kinds of breaths you breathe each day. Begin by bringing awareness to what kind of breathing happens in your ventral, sympathetic, and dorsal states. Experiment with different kinds of breath. Notice how each impacts your autonomic state. Identify breaths that are mobilizing, calming, disconnecting, and connecting.

• Find the places you feel breath moving in your body. Some of the common places to find your breath are the abdomen, chest, heart, throat, just under the breastbone, in the side ribs, and in your lower back. Choose two places and put one hand on each. As you inhale and exhale, feel your breath moving between your hands. Find places that offer an easy pathway to feel the breath flowing between your two hands.

• Create a mantra. The use of mantras is common in mindfulness practice and is a way to bring focused intention to your breath. Find a word or a phrase for each inhalation and exhalation that brings awareness to the feeling of energy rising and falling (mobilize, calm), the sense of inward and outward connection (tune in, reach out), and moving between action and rest (attentive, peaceful). Honor the ways your autonomic nervous system and breath are interconnected. Let your breath and body guide you in finding your own words and phrases.

• Take breath outside your body and add movement (arm movement or full body movement) to follow your inhalation and exhalation. Notice how your movements change when the quality of your breath changes. Find a pattern that feels restorative and create a daily practice of moving with your breath.

THE POWER OF A SIGH

Sighing resets the respiratory system, affecting our physiological state and impacting the story that emerges. Humans sigh many times an hour and those spontaneous sighs are a sign our autonomic nervous systems are looking for regulation. We can intentionally sigh to momentarily interrupt a survival state or to appreciate the experience of being anchored in safety. Become aware of the times you spontaneously sigh as your system looks for regulation. Make a practice of noticing. Spend a moment actively appreciating the wisdom of your biology.

- Experiment with different sighs—deep or shallow, loud or soft, through the nose or mouth. With each sigh, look for subtle shifts in your state and thoughts.

- Connect with a moment of dorsal collapse and breathe a sigh of despair.

- Move into a moment of sympathetic mobilization and breathe a sigh of frustration.

- End in the regulated energy of ventral and breathe a sigh of relief that you have found your way here. Linger in this place of safety and connection and breathe a sigh of contentment.

- Create a habit of bringing a sigh to a difficult situation. Make a practice of turning to a sigh when you are feeling caught in dorsal or sympathetic survival energy. The small interruption can begin the return to regulation.

- Sigh to deepen a state of regulation and nourish a story of well-being.

TOUCHING SAFETY

We routinely engage in self-touch many times during the day. We put a hand on our heart when we're moved by a moment and hold our head when we're distressed. We wring our hands and massage our tired feet. Touch can activate our survival responses and help us anchor in safety.

Experiment with self-regulation through self-touch. Explore the following questions and use the Touch Map to record what you discover.

Self Touch Map

Ventral	deepens	
	activates	
Sympathetic	shifts	
	activates	
Dorsal	shifts	
	activates	

- What kind of self-touch invites a sense of safety and regulation? Evokes sympathetic distress? Elicits dorsal numbing?

- What ways of touching deepens your sense of safety and what helps you shift out of states of survival?

- Explore different ways of touching (firm, soft, steady, intermittent, moving, static) and places for touching.

• Combining words with touch is a way to deepen the experience. Pair words with the self-touch that helps you anchor in safety and regulation.

ENERGY AND ACTIONS

Activities that shape the autonomic nervous system fall along a scale of passive to active. There are times when thinking about moving, remembering a connection with a friend, or simply looking up toward the sky is the right choice, and other times when we need to act, put our bodies in motion, or head out into the world and seek social connection. We want a continuum of choices so we can match an action to the energy we have access to in the moment. We need resources that bring a return of energy when the dorsal vagal immobilizing collapse is present, ways to organize our energy when feeling the frenetic activity of the sympathetic state, and actions that deepen

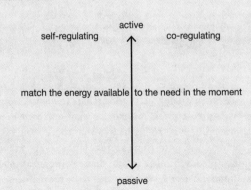

Name of State

active

self-regulating   co-regulating

match the energy available to the need in the moment

passive

the feeling of regulation when anchored in the safety of ventral vagal.

- Complete a map for each state. Use the left side to identify self-regulating actions and the right side to identify co-regulating actions.

- Label your state in the box at the top of the Energy and Actions map. You can use the biological name (dorsal, sympathetic, ventral) or name it in a way that has meaning for you.

- For sympathetic and dorsal states, move along the line between passive and active and identify actions that take you in the direction of a return to the ventral state of regulation.

- For your ventral state, move along the line between passive and active and identify actions that deepen your experience of safety and connection.

Your Energy and Actions Maps offer an easy way to engage with a resource that is in the range of energy that fits your needs in the moment. Review your maps and update them as you discover new resources.

DEVELOPING A RESOURCE MENU

Every day we read about ways to find calm, get healthy, and practice self-care and yet often those suggestions don't seem to fit for us. Rather than following someone else's prescription, we can develop our own menu of choices following the principle that there is no right way or wrong way to come to regulation. Our exploration is guided by tuning in and discovering what meets our autonomic needs. We create our resource menu based not on what someone else tells us is helpful but by listening to our own internal experience. What nourishes one nervous system may be a cue of danger to another. What feels like too much of a challenge in this moment may be just right at another time. When we create a personalized menu, with multiple pathways, we build a more flexible pattern of response, and our autonomic nervous systems anchor in safety more reliably and easily.

A resource menu lists a variety of options so we can find the way to meet our need in the moment.

- Decide how you want to write your menu. You might want to type a simple list or you might want to create a colorful chart.

- Include all the practices that help you find the way to the ventral state and anchor there, then arrange them in a way that works for you. You could sort them in categories of the three states, things you do on your own or with others, practices that take you out into the world and ones that you can do at home, or the amount of time and effort they require.

- Use your menu to create a plan for the day. See what activities you are pulled toward as you look at the day ahead.

- Turn to your menu when you need to reach for a resource in the moment.

PLANNING AN AUTONOMIC ADVENTURE

What do you pack to take with you when you leave the house? Water? A snack? Your wallet? Your phone? What are the essential items you need to feel ready to head out into the world? Much like deciding what to pack when we leave the house, we can choose objects, create images, and set intentions that help us stay anchored in regulation as we head into a challenging moment or simply out into the flow of our day.

Consider the day ahead. What will help you move through the day from a place of regulation?

- Look for an object you can carry with you that holds the energy of safety and regulation. (I have a favorite beach stone I often put in my pocket.)

- See yourself anchored in your ventral state.

- Write a statement reminding you that your biology includes the state of ventral safety and connection, and it is always available.

When you know your day will include a moment that feels a bit challenging, pay extra attention to the objects, images, and intentions that will keep you anchored in safety. Whether you're heading into an ordinary day or a difficult day, recognize what you want to have within reach and bring that awareness into action.

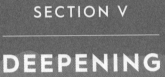

SECTION V

DEEPENING

■ SMALL AND OFTEN ■

The autonomic nervous system learns about the world through experience, and while early experiences shape the nervous system, ongoing experiences reshape it. Just as the brain is continually changing in response to our daily experiences, our autonomic nervous systems are likewise engaged. Change is not an event but rather a lifelong process and autonomic reorganization is ongoing. The way to autonomic change is by doing small things over and over. Incremental change leads to transformational change. Small, and often fleeting, ventral moments accumulate and compound over time building a new foundation of well-being making it easier to resist the pull of old patterns. The hope-filled message from Polyvagal Theory is that regularly repeated experiences shape our nervous systems in new ways. In times of regulation and safety, we anchor in the ventral state and move through the world with a sense of well-being. On the days that feel overwhelming and regulation feels impossible, we look for micro-moments of safety and connection. Both experiences build and deepen pathways to safety.

The steps of discovering, doing, and deepening guide us into a stronger, more predictable connection with safety and regulation.

Discovering

Our autonomic nervous systems inherently know the way back home to safety and regulation, and we each find our own ways to enter into that experience. We personalize the practice by trying out different ways of connecting to the ventral state and then creating a combination of practices that help us safely reach for regulation.

Doing

With patience and persistence, we strengthen our connection to ventral safety and regulation. For many of us patience is a challenging quality. Patience is only possible from a state of ventral regulation, so even remembering the need for patience is part of the practice. With persistence, we keep coming into awareness of the power of old patterns and returning to the simple practices that bring connection to safety.

Deepening

Small moments move our nervous systems toward a tipping point. Micro-moments lead to a larger change. New stories take root. Behind the scenes the autonomic nervous system, through habitual patterns of response, generates stories. Our sympathetic and dorsal survival energies create stories of scarcity. As we deepen into new patterns and feel the solidity of the ventral vagal state of safety, we hear a story of abundance.

■ THE POWER OF GLIMMERS ■

Glimmers are micro-moments of ventral experience that routinely appear in everyday life, yet frequently go unnoticed. A glimmer could be seeing a friendly face, hearing a soothing sound, or noticing something enjoyable in the environment. These tiny moments gently yet significantly shape our systems toward well-being. Glimmers are easily overlooked because the human brain is wired to pay more attention to negative events than positive ones. But once we learn to look for glimmers, we find they are all around us and we begin to look for more. Recognizing glimmers doesn't discount our distress or disavow the ways we are suffering. Glimmers offer a reminder that our nervous systems can hold both dysregulation and regulation— that our days can be filled with difficulty, and we can also feel a spark of ventral safety. Sometimes simply navigating the day ahead feels like an autonomic challenge. These are *glimmer days*, when noticing micro-moments of ventral vagal energy can help us stay regulated and ready for connection.

While it's lovely to keep track of our glimmers in an intentional way and certainly this enhances the reshaping process, the magic of glimmers is that even when we can't hold them in ongoing awareness, the micro-moments accumulate and move us along the path toward physical and psychological well-being. There is a moment when we feel something shift. We feel a tiny change in our body. We notice a thought that holds a hint of hope. A micro-moment may make its way into our awareness for a fleeting moment and then quickly disappear. Take a moment and appreciate the way your nervous system gathers glimmers, adding them up one by one until a threshold is crossed and something in your world feels just a bit different.

Glimmers appear in many ways. A hummingbird taught me about unpredictably predictable glimmers and that they can bring a moment of magic. He appeared one day to drink from the flowers on my deck and became a regular visitor. He often flew to the screen door and hovered there. We would share a look before he flew off again. He was unpredictable in the times he showed up and constant in that he continued to appear. So, he became my unpredictably predictable glimmer. I'm used to thinking that glimmers bring a spark of joy. My hummingbird friend taught me that glimmers come in many different flavors. He showed me that a glimmer can bring a moment of magic.

Glimmers are a reminder that ventral energy is always around waiting to be noticed and nourish our nervous systems.

- What are the cues that you have found a glimmer? What happens in your body that lets you know you are in a glimmer moment? What do you feel, think, or do when you feel that spark of ventral energy? Once you discover the cues, use them to look for glimmers as you move through your day.
- Notice all the different kinds of feelings your glimmers bring as you go through your day.
- Glimmers happen regularly, but because they are micromoments you need to be on the lookout for them. Look for predictable glimmer moments in specific places, with particular people, at certain times. Find the ways glimmers routinely appear. See, stop, and appreciate your glimmers. Create an easy way to acknowledge a glimmer as it happens. You might repeat a simple phrase or make

a small movement (perhaps your hand on your heart or a finger pointing toward the glimmer) each time you find a glimmer.

- Keep track of your glimmers. Write about the predictable times and places you find a glimmer as well as the unexpected moments. Share your glimmers. You might text your glimmers to a friend or make talking about daily glimmers a family ritual.

- Set a glimmer intention. The intention I often use is, "I am ready to find the glimmers on my path today."

PRACTICING SAVORING

Savoring is a practice of capturing and deepening the ventral moments that inevitably emerge as we move through the day. Because this practice takes advantage of naturally occurring moments, it is easy to incorporate into the flow of the day. Sometimes negative thoughts intrude and interrupt the ability to stay in the ventral experience and, rather than resourcing, the practice of savoring becomes distressing. It's not an uncommon experience to think you don't deserve to feel this, it's dangerous to feel good, or something bad will happen if you stop and appreciate the moment. When this happens, start slowly with five or ten seconds, and build toward twenty or thirty. Find the amount of time that supports your ability to stay anchored in the ventral state. Each micro-moment shapes your system. Over time, your ability to savor will build to the 20–30 seconds that defines a savoring experience.

- Notice a ventral moment and focus your attention on it.

- Hold the moment in your awareness and stay with it for 20–30 seconds.

- Feel your body anchored in ventral and listen to the story that accompanies your savoring.

- Ventral moments are common occurrences in everyday life and we often move right by them. Be on the lookout for moments to savor during the day. Stopping to notice and taking 30 seconds to mark the moment is a simple but powerful way to deepen your ability to anchor in safety.

- At the end of the day take a moment to reflect on the day and look for moments you may have missed.

- If you want, invite a friend to savor with you. When you share your moments, you feel them come alive again.

SIFTING

SIFTing is a way to bring a ventral experience that you have already experienced back into awareness, re-experience it, and create a regulating resource. In the SIFT practice, the four elements of body sensation, image, emotional feeling, and thought are used to bring a ventral memory back to life and relive it.

- On a piece of paper or an index card write the letters for your SIFT.

- Think of a ventral experience you would like to revisit. Return to that experience and feel what happens in your body—what you see, feel, and think as you remember the moment.

- Identify the element that is most alive and accessible to you (body sensation, image, feeling, thought), and write a short statement next to its letter describing it.
- Move through the other elements and write statements describing each of them.
- Give your SIFT a title. Read the title and the four statements of your SIFT and take time to re-experience that ventral moment.

Make a practice of finding moments to SIFT and create a collection of them. When you are feeling a need for ventral regulation, read one of your SIFTs and revisit that moment to return to regulation.

Examples of a SIFT

Title—My Beach

S:	The feeling of warm sand under my feet
I:	Long stretch of beach, gentle waves, no other people, white clouds in a blue sky
F:	Happy
T:	I'm home

Title—Anchored in Safety

S:	Feeling the solidity of my bare feet on the ground
I:	Standing in the sunshine, eyes closed, face turned toward the sky
F:	Content
T:	The world is welcoming

TIME FOR PLAY

Play is possible when we are anchored in safety. Our collective and personal experiences along with the state of the world challenge our ability to play. Being playful might feel like a luxury, frivolous, or even disrespectful in difficult times, yet play helps us see new perspectives and cope with challenges in new ways. Moments of playfulness are important ways we shape our systems toward increased regulation. We are serious beings, problem solvers wanting to make sense of the world, but we are also playful beings who want to let go of our problems, if only for a moment.

Playfulness is an essential ingredient of well-being and a quality that can be enhanced and become part of our daily lived experience. Take time to get to know yourself as a playful person.

- What are the conditions that invite you into a moment of play? Remember moments when you found joy in play and notice where, when, and with whom your sense of playfulness emerges.

- What are the barriers to play? Think about what makes play feel unsafe and identify where, when, and with whom your sense of playfulness disappears.

- Assess your responses by noticing what happens in your nervous system. When you think about where, when, and with whom, notice how each land for you. What state becomes active?

Once you know what supports you in being playful, find ways to bring more of those opportunities into your daily experience. Even if you think you've lost the ability to be playful, research tells us that playfulness is a quality that can be enhanced, and moments of playfulness are an essential ingredient in well-being. The sense of who you are as a playful person changes over time. Some barriers resolve while others appear. We find joy in both predictable ways and unexpected moments. Be curious, continue to learn what supports you in being playful, and invite more of those elements into your life.

NOURISHED IN STILLNESS

When we find our way to stillness, we discover comfort in moments of quiet, gather information from self-reflection, join with others in wordless connection, and are present to the joy of intimate experiences. This resourcing state of being is a complicated and challenging physiological process. The vagus with its two branches can bring us alive in joy, passion, ease, and calm, or take us into a survival state of disconnection, numbing, and collapse. It is only when these two vagal pathways, the ancient energy of immobilization and the new energy of connection join together that we can experience stillness without fear.

Stillness is a way to rest and renew. Yet sometimes, instead of feeling nurtured by stillness, the beginning of calm can bring cues of danger and a sense of vulnerability. As our autonomic nervous systems begin to move from action to quiet, we might feel our sympathetic nervous system reacting with mobilizing energy or feel pulled into dorsal vagal collapse. It may be helpful to remember that even when we have found our way to stillness, we are still moving. We can feel our heart beating, our chest and abdomen rising and falling as we breathe. Beneath awareness, our blood is circulating; our lungs and diaphragm are moving. Take a moment and move slowly from motion to rest while tracking your autonomic response.

It's important to listen to our autonomic nervous systems as we consider what brings us safely into stillness. If we bring curiosity to identifying elements that add safety to the experience, we can find our way to the people and places where we receive the benefits of moments of quiet.

We each have our own words to describe our experiences of stillness. Common words include stillness, quiet, rest, and solitude. Before we begin to practice stillness, find the word that fits for you.

Explore the following questions to discover where your moments of stillness can be found.

- Who are the people in your life with whom you feel safe to be still? Which relationships includes stillness? What are the qualities of those connections that invite you into stillness?

- Where are the places in your everyday life you can find a moment to be safely still? Where are the places that bring you a feeling of restfulness? Is there a place in your home, in your neighborhood, a place you pass by regularly? Is there a special place you visited that comes alive in your memory? Attend to the qualities of the places that bring you a rhythm of rest: location, size and shape of the space, colors, sounds, and textures. Make a list of the combination of qualities you've identified. Listen to your autonomic nervous system as you explore environments that offer an opportunity for stillness. Go out and find places that offer those. Look for places that are easy to return to and where you can predictably find a moment of stillness. Create your own space, incorporating the qualities you identified that support you in resting in a moment of stillness.

- When are the times when you can most easily find stillness? Is there a time of day that invites you into stillness? Or a certain day of the week? Is there an activity you engage in that offers time for stillness?

- How do you know when you need a moment of stillness? What cues does your autonomic nervous system send you? Tune in and listen to the cues your autonomic nervous system is sending.

- Try using imagery to illustrate your experiences of stillness. Create an image that includes all the elements that invite you to rest. Take time to experiment as you fill in the details. When it feels complete, enter your image. See yourself in the picture and find your way to stillness.

- Feel your body moving from motion to rest. Listen to the story that emerges. As you begin to explore moving into stillness, feelings and memories that have been out of conscious awareness may reappear and present a challenge. If that happens see what details you can add to your imagery to promote more safety and support you in entering a micro-moment of stillness.

Through all the different ways of practicing coming into stillness, we begin to shape our autonomic nervous systems in new ways, and our capacity to be safely still deepens.

EVERYDAY AWE

Awe is a state of wonder, curiosity, reverence, and deep appreciation. It exists along a continuum of ordinary to extraordinary, from everyday moments that are awe-inspiring to the profound moments when we are awestruck. In a moment of awe, we feel both small and connected to something much larger than ourselves, and this transforms how we experience the world. Awe reminds us that we are part of humankind, intricately connected to the world.

Moments of awe are all around us. People, nature, architecture, the arts, spiritual experiences, and inexplicable events have the potential to elicit feelings of awe. Where are your moments of awe each day that are waiting to be discovered?

- Everyday awe moments are abundant in daily life. How do you recognize them? Get to know the cues from your body and mind that you are experiencing a moment of awe.

- Consider your everyday awe experiences. Certain people inspire awe. Who are those people for you? They may be people you know and have a relationship with or people you know of and admire. Places, the architecture of a particular structure, and natural formations in the outside world regularly offer experiences of awe. Art and music predictably activate awe. Spiritual experiences are awe-filled. Notice where in your daily life you find awe.

- Be open to the inexplicable events that unexpectedly appear. Let go of the need to understand and explain those moments and let in the experience of awe.

- Although the state of awe is often unexpected, it can also be intentionally inspired. Look for the small moments of awe that are easily repeatable.

- Find your awe environments—the places you can easily return to and experience a moment of awe—and return to them regularly.

Create a practice of watching for moments of awe as you move through your daily routine. Identify the predictable moments and appreciate the unexpected ones. When we notice the everyday moments of awe all around us, we deepen our sense of well-being.

▪ DEVELOPING A NEW RHYTHM ▪ OF REGULATION

Habitual autonomic patterns work in the background, bringing a familiar rhythm to our everyday experiences. When those patterns arise from a flexible autonomic nervous system, ventral vagal energy supports our ability to meet challenges and move through the day safely and successfully. This is a rhythm to deepen and celebrate. Ongoing activation of sympathetic or dorsal energy creates rigid response patterns, and with rigidity comes suffering. Here we need to gently shake up the system, interrupt the engrained patterns of protection, and enliven our ventral vagal capacities. As we add practices that help us anchor in safety, we create a new rhythm of regulation. We move out of the survival responses of the sympathetic and dorsal vagal systems into a foundation of ventral vagal regulation. Using the framework of the autonomic hierarchy, we learn to "rise to the occasion." From that place, we can weather the common, inevitable times when we are pulled into defense and still feel anchored in our ventral state of safety, held in a story of abundance.

Setting intentions is a common practice to support making changes. We think about something we are trying to achieve and create a statement to help us reach that goal. Unfortunately, our brains and bodies are often not in agreement about the pathway to change and because of that we struggle to realize an intention. When our brains and our nervous systems are not on the same page, our nervous systems will have the last word. When our nervous systems are included, the intention setting process becomes a collaboration between our bodies and brains. Our brains often overestimate our capacity, and our nervous systems can help temper the expectations so we can be successful. Each small success builds confidence and strengthens the connection between body and brain.

An intention has to bring the right degree of challenge. Too much and we move into a survival response. Not enough and our nervous system won't recognize the invitation to repattern. To set an autonomic intention:

- Choose a focus for your intention. What are you interested in shaping in a new way?
- Write your intention, read it, and then say it out loud. Each way of exploring the intention is important. What is your nervous system's response? Does it feel too bland, too big, or just right?
- Rewrite the intention until your brain and body are on the same page—when the words of your intention activate a ventral inspired readiness to engage.

A good way to begin is by asking yourself these three general questions and writing an autonomically guided intention for each.

- Where do I want my autonomic patterns to take me?
- What do I want change?
- What do I want to deepen?

SECTION VI

REFLECTING

▪ THE PATHS WE TRAVEL ▪

Our bodies and brains are intimately connected. Autonomic state and psychological story combine to bring us experiences that are sometimes nourishing and sometimes painful. Through the art of reflection, we can shape our systems in the direction of safety and connection. Reflection invites awareness of where we are and where we have been and leads to thinking about where we might be heading. Making time to slow down and become curious helps us recognize the many states and state changes that we naturally experience while navigating the demands of the day and appreciate the autonomic pathways that we have traveled. When we are anchored in a ventral state, we connect with our observing selves. We see individual moments and can take a step back and see the larger picture of how those moments fit together to form a whole. We come into a wider and deeper understanding of the autonomic shape of our days.

With awareness of the flow of our autonomic states during a day, we access a rich stream of autonomic information. We can track the individual moments that catch our attention and put them on an autonomic timeline to see how, when they are linked together, each individual story becomes part of a larger narrative.

FOUR MAP TRACKING

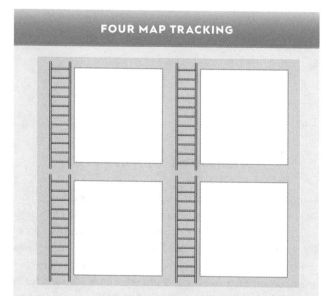

This practice uses four ladder boxes to bring attention to the autonomic path we traveled in the course of our day. You might decide to schedule specific times to listen in, choose to pause during your day when you notice a state you want to stop and attend to, or even fill in the boxes as an end-of-the-day reflection.

- First, mark your place on the ladder and then use the box to describe the moment. You can write a story, use single words, draw a picture, or just play with color. Find the way you want to record and remember. As you fill in each box, decide how you want to represent the moment.

- When you have completed your four maps, take time to review the four moments and see where your nervous system has taken you.

SOUP OF THE DAY

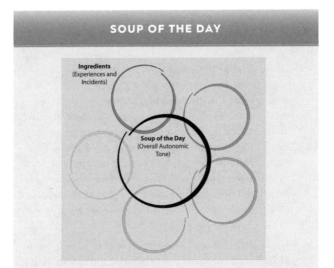

The Soup of the Day practice offers a way to reflect on our autonomic experiences at the end of the day. In creating our soup, we identify an overall flavor of the day and reflect on the individual experiences that are woven together to create that. This exercise draws on our ventral energy to allow us to step back, observe, and reflect on the autonomic pathways we traveled over the course of the day.

Imagine your autonomic experiences are like a bowl of homemade soup, an ever-changing soup of the day. The ingredients bring a variety of flavors, and the final product is distinctive. Your overall autonomic state (the soup) is flavored by the influence of ventral vagal, sympathetic, and dorsal vagal energies (the ingredients). Using the soup metaphor, some flavors are intense (sudden and extreme state shifts), and some bring milder hints of seasoning (the nuance of movement within a state).

WRITING YOUR RECIPE

- You can write the recipe for your soup of the day in two ways: name the soup first, then look for the ingredients, or find the ingredients then see what soup they produce. If you have a strong sense of your overall autonomic tone, begin with naming that in the center circle. Then, explore the medley of experiences that make up that sense and place those in the outer circles. Alternatively, you may clearly remember experiences from the day and choose to add those to the outer circles; then see what the overall tone is and identify that in the inner circle.

- Using either process, it is important to look for not only the intense experiences but also the more mildly activating events. Look both for the experiences that are similar and may support a theme and the outlier experiences that add diverse energies. As you fill in your soup recipes, you will notice the ways moments of ventral, sympathetic, and dorsal activation create a unique overall tone depending on their frequency, duration, and intensity.

- When you are finished creating your soup, give it a name (e.g., Spicy Ventral Gumbo, Fiery Chowder, Soup that Needs Spice).

When we engage in this process over time, we build a habit of autonomic reflection and awareness of the blend of autonomic states that come together to create our daily experience.

▪ PIE CHARTS ▪

When we reflect on the day through the lens of our nervous system, we recognize ventral, sympathetic, and dorsal moments and see that our overall experience is a result of the contributions of each. Looking at the relationship between states and the relative amount of time spent in each state helps us see beyond a moment to the bigger picture of our daily experience. Using a pie chart, ventral, sympathetic, and dorsal experiences are seen as part of an integrated autonomic system, and the feeling of the day comes alive in shape and color.

CREATE A PIE CHART

- Draw a circle and divide it into "slices" for ventral, sympathetic, and dorsal, adjusting the size of each slice to represent how much time you spent in that state. How big is each piece of the pie?
- Once you have divided your pie, fill in each piece with colors, words, images, or shapes to illustrate your experience of that state.
- When you've finished, reflect on your chart and give your day a name (e.g., Happy Day, Stormy Weather, Lost Time)

The end of the day is a good time to reflect on the flow of states we naturally experience while navigating life's demands. Collect a series of charts to get a sense of your autonomic experience over time. See what patterns are in place and what is emerging.

WRITING AUTONOMIC HAIKU

Haiku is a form of poetry made up of three lines and seventeen syllables. The first line has five syllables, the second has seven syllables, and the third, again, has five syllables. Haiku captures a moment in time with just a few words. Writing a haiku invites you to identify the essence of an autonomic moment. You can write a haiku that represents a moment in each state, reflects an experience of being held in your regulated system, illustrates sympathetic and dorsal survival responses, or brings to life the way you move between states. The only rules for writing a haiku are the number of lines and syllables. This is an invitation to play with words and see what emerges.

> No energy. Stuck.
> Gray clouds. Rain falling. Gloomy.
> A rainbow. Magic!

> Down the dorsal drain.
> Moving up to mobilize.
> Finding the way home.

> Walking by the sea.
> The sand and waves nourish me.
> I am filled with peace.

LOVING-KINDNESS MEDITATION

Loving-kindness meditation is an ancient practice that focuses on self-generated feelings of love, compassion, and goodwill toward oneself and others. Loving-kindness meditation engages the power of the ventral system first through self-compassion and then by offering compassion to others. The traditional four phrases of loving-kindness meditation are, "May I be happy. May I be healthy. May I be safe. May I live with ease." Some variation of these four phrases has been used for centuries. Using the focus of the four traditional phrases—happiness, health, safety, ease—this practice invites you to find the words that are most personally meaningful. Let your ventral state guide you.

- Look at the four categories (happy, healthy, safe, and living with ease) through the language of the autonomic nervous system. Find the words that you would use and write your own four phrases. Here is an example: May I find glimmers every day. May I be nourished by the flow of ventral vagal energy. May I be filled with a neuroception of safety. May I live in the rhythm of a regulated nervous system.

- Say your phrases out loud. Listen to the words and feel how they land in your system. You will know you have found the right words when you feel a deep connection to your ventral system. Say the phrases to yourself ("May I"). Then send the phrases to others ("May you") beginning with someone you feel safe and connected to, then a neutral person, then someone with whom you may have an unrepaired rupture, and finally to all living beings.

- You might want to share your four phrases with someone else. First, say your phrases to the other person and then ask them to read the phrases back to you. Notice what happens when you offer and receive your unique phrases. Track your autonomic response to the experience of first offering compassion and then receiving compassion.

MEASURING CHANGE

Change is not an event but rather a lifelong process and autonomic reorganization is ongoing. In the midst of daily living, it is easy to miss the small moments that mark the beginning of change. Listening to the subtleties of autonomic change is a good way to look at the autonomic path we have traveled. A regular practice brings attention to the small shifts that highlight the ways our patterns are shifting, and our systems are reorganizing. The relationship between our states changes in small ways throughout the day. Each shift adds up, turning these micro-moments of change into predictable new pathways within our nervous system. A daily practice of stopping to notice these small shifts brings attention to the autonomic changes happening.

- Review the day and identify different ways your autonomic nervous system responded. You might notice a slightly less intense response to an event or an easier recovery into regulation. Maybe you recognize a different kind of response—sympathetic mobilization in place of a dorsal vagal collapse or a moment of ventral vagal connection instead of a move to fight. It's equally important to attend to what didn't happen. The absence of a reaction is also a good measure that a response pattern is changing and that your system is moving toward regulation.

- Fill in the following sentences to reflect on the shifts that are happening.

   Instead of my expected sympathetic mobilization, I . . .

   Instead of my familiar dorsal vagal disconnection, I . . .

> I notice I am more . . .
> I notice I am less . . .
>
> • Return to the sentences periodically to track what is changing. As small changes begin to add up, new autonomic patterns take root.

▪ NAVIGATING IN A NEW WAY ▪

Learning how to move through the world with new autonomic rhythms can be daunting. We are in a space between old patterns and new pathways. When "before" no longer feels true and "after" has not quite made itself known, we can feel unsure of how to engage with others and move through our daily experiences. In this time of transition, we need to hold on to the ventral pathways that we reliably travel and tend to the new patterns that are taking root.

Humans are meaning-making beings, automatically pulled toward story. Working with practices that help us anchor in safety brings us to re-storying. As we integrate new patterns, we move out of our old stories and head toward new ones. This transition often brings discomfort, and we can easily be pulled back into old familiar stories about ourselves and the world. The re-storying process disrupts the habit of listening to an old story and encourages the development of a new one. Re-storying invites us to become active authors of our own autonomic adventures.

We are all on an autonomic journey—an adventure that includes survival and safety, protection and connection. It's important to see the arc of our story—to see where we were, where we are, and where we are heading. Transition comes from the Latin word *transire* meaning to go across and often refers to the process, not the end result. As we write our autonomic story, we look for the internal and external transitions on our before, now, and later timeline.

Follow the path of your autonomic story. Write and/or illustrate what stands out for you.

- Where have I been?
- Where am I now?
- Where am I going?

AUTONOMIC MEDITATIONS

Old Vagus

Rest your gaze on the image of the vagus—cranial nerve X, the longest cranial nerve, aptly named *the wanderer* . . .

Follow the vagal pathways from the base of your skull down to their roots deep in your viscera . . .

Sense into the branches of these fibers . . .

Feel the flow of energy up and down the vagal highway . . .

Savor the familiarity of this embodied home . . .

An Integrated System

Begin by making the turn from outward awareness to inner experience. Close your eyes if that feels comfortable or simply soften your gaze. Allow yourself to disconnect from the world around you and connect inside as you begin your exploration of the qualities of an integrated autonomic nervous system. This is the system in balance, where the three streams of autonomic experience join their energies to work in cooperation, bringing health, growth, and restoration. Move into connection with these regulating energies . . .

Begin in the ancient dorsal vagal branch, the part of your autonomic nervous system that lies below the diaphragm. Envision your diaphragm, the muscle at the bottom of your ribs separating your chest from your abdomen. Then begin to move slowly downward following your digestive tract. Feel into your stomach, your intestines, sense the process of digestion that brings nutrients to nourish you. This is the realm of the dorsal vagus, slow, deliberate, steady. Take a moment to feel this ancient beat . . .

Now travel upward to the sympathetic branch and find movement and energy. Feel your spinal cord and then sense into the middle of your back. Feel your sympathetic nervous system circulating your blood, influencing your heartbeat, making moment-to-moment adjustments to your body temperature. The rhythm here awakens you. Sense the stirring of energy. Soak in this invitation toward movement . . .

And now to find the newest branch, the ventral vagus. Return to your diaphragm and move up to your heart, to your lungs, to your throat. This is the system of breath, beat, and sound. Sense a sigh of relief. Feel the rhythm of your heart and the vibration in your throat. Continue upward to your face, eyes, and ears. Find the energy of engagement. Feel the pull toward connection. Allow that energy to build and fill you . . .

From this place, tune in to the gentle ways the ventral vagus watches over your system, bringing regulating energy allowing the sympathetic and dorsal vagal branches to do their work. Bathe in this experience of homeostasis . . .

Feeling the Face-Heart Connection

Close your eyes if that feels safe or simply soften your gaze. Place your hands at the base of your skull. Here in the brain stem is the evolutionary origin of your Social Engagement System. Focus your attention on the place where your brain stem meets your spinal cord, the space where five cranial nerves come together to form the pathways of your face-heart connection. This is the hub of your Social Engagement System. Rest here for a moment. Sense the beginnings of your quest for connection.

Now, move your hands placing one hand on the side of your face and the other over your heart. Feel the flow of energy moving between your hands, traveling from your face to your heart and your heart to your face. Follow this pathway in both directions. Explore the ways your face-heart connection searches for contact and signals safety. Sense this system reaching out into the world, listening for sounds of welcome, looking for friendly faces, turning and tilting your head seeking safety. Feel your heart joining in the search. And now feel this system broadcasting signals of safety . . . your eyes, your voice, your head movements inviting others into connection. Your heart sending its own welcome.

Move between the two experiences of sending and searching. Broadcasting and receiving. Take time to savor the pathways of your face-heart connection.

Anchored in Ventral

Just as an anchor holds a ship safely, you can anchor in your ventral vagal state. Feel yourself rooted in the energy of safety that the ventral vagal system offers.

Your breath is full. Each exhalation moves you along the vagal pathway that supports safety and connection. Your heart rate is variable. This arrhythmic beat brings well-being. You are being held in the autonomic safety circuit. Your afferent, body to brain vagal pathway sends messages of stability and the returning, efferent, brain to body pathway creates the story of safety. From this foundation of ventral vagal energy, with the sense of your anchor firmly planted in your ventral vagal system, you can safely begin the journey to explore your sympathetic nervous system and dorsal vagal responses.

Reach into the mobilized energy of the sympathetic nervous system. Your breath changes. Your heart rate speeds up. You want to move. Your thoughts swirl. Envision the sympathetic sea and the energy that moves here mobilizing your system toward action. Perhaps you can feel the wind blowing, disturbing the sea, and sense the waves—rolling breakers, crashing surf, even a tsunami. Notice you can safely navigate this sympathetic storm. You are tethered to your ventral vagal system. Remember your anchor is deeply dug into the firm ground of ventral vagal regulation.

Return to where you first set your anchor. Sense the regulating energies of your breath and heartbeat. Feel a flow of warmth in your chest. Your ventral vagal system is sending you signals of safety.

Dip into the dorsal vagal state. This is not the dorsal dive that can take you out of present time awareness and into numbness. This is an experimental dipping of your toe into the feeling of disconnection. Energy begins to drain from your body and everything starts to slow down. You feel a restriction of movement. Titrate this

experience bringing active remembrance of your connection to your ventral vagal state—the place you set
your anchor. Feel your ventral vagal regulating energies
controlling the depth and the speed of the dorsal vagal
descent. You are moving along a slope not plummeting
into space. Your anchor is secure, holding your place in
ventral vagal regulation, allowing you to safely examine
the dorsal vagal experience.

Come back to where you started in ventral vagal regulation. Return to where you first set your anchor. Reflect
on the ways you can meet your sympathetic nervous system and dorsal vagal responses when guided by your
autonomic safety circuit.

Map, Track, Honor, Nourish

Close your eyes or simply soften your gaze and settle into
comfortable awareness of your autonomic nervous system. Bring your autonomic map to life. See your map in
your mind's eye, and find your place on it. Explore the
terrain. Where has your autonomic journey taken you
today? Retrace the path you've traveled. See individual
moments marked along the way.

Take a moment to reflect on those experiences. Notice
the shape of your route . . . the directions your autonomic
pathway has taken you.

See large-scale state changes illustrated in steep
angles.

Notice the nuanced shifts found in soft curves.

Appreciate the path your nervous system has taken
in service of your safety. The path you have traveled
to this moment in time—to this particular place on
your map.

Take a moment to listen to the autonomic story your map is telling.

Anchored and Open

Close your eyes or simply soften your gaze—whichever feels right to you in this moment. Begin to move from outward awareness to inner connection. Allow yourself to disconnect from the demands of the world around you. Sense into the experience of being anchored in your autonomic nervous system, grounded, firmly planted in regulation.

Invite an image to illustrate your experience. See if there's a movement that accompanies the image. Take time to let the image and movement emerge. Come to rest in the safety of your nervous system.

Now begin to feel the way your anchor holds you in safety and regulation and supports you in having the freedom to move—to respond to changing conditions—to open to the world around you. Appreciate the experience of being safely held and venturing out without becoming adrift. Of being anchored and open.

Invite an image to illustrate this experience. The experience of being anchored in safety and open to the world around you. See if there is a movement that accompanies the image. Invite a series of movements that acknowledge the dual experience of being anchored and open. Take time and allow your images and movements to come to life.

From this place of embodied knowing—connected with your biology, engaged with the images and movements that bring to life the experience of being anchored and open—imagine standing in the midst of challenges with equilibrium able to move with ease in all directions, while staying anchored in safety and regulation.

See the many pathways and possibilities that appear. Sense into the experience of exploring with safety. Celebrate knowing that you have an anchor in regulation.

And from that anchor, you can be open to discovery, to new experiences, to new stories. As you prepare to make the journey from inward attention to outward awareness, take a moment to send a message of gratitude.

Safely Still

Close your eyes or soften your gaze, whichever feels right for you in this moment. As you begin to move inside, make the intention to explore the feeling of quiet and experience a moment of being safely still.

Come into connection with your vagus nerve. Feel the ancient energy of immobilization and the new energy of connection moving together, two branches of one nerve joining to create an experience of stillness without fear.

Sense the fibers of these two vagal pathways traveling together as you begin to move from action to quiet. Feel your wise, social vagus reassuring your ancient, protective vagus that, in this moment, it is safe to become still. Sense your system begin to enter into stillness without fear.

Pause in the stillness for a moment or a micro-moment. Feel the blend of your two vagal circuits. Within the ventral vagal story of safety, your dorsal vagus is bringing stillness. And from this state where is it safe to be still, you are open to reflection, ready to sit in silence and savor intimate connection.

Benevolence

Close your eyes or simply soften your gaze. Find the place inside your body where you sense the stirring of ventral vagal energy. This may be your heart, your chest, your face, behind your eyes, or somewhere else unique to your system. Feel the place where your energy of kindness is born. Settle into that space for a moment.

Join in the flow of ventral vagal energy as it moves throughout your body. Maybe there is a sense of warmth spreading. Perhaps your heart feels as if it is expanding, or your chest feels full. There might be a tingling in your eyes or a tightness in your throat. Take a moment to get to know your own personal experience of this ventral vagal flow. Stop and savor this state.

Now imagine actively using this energy in the service of healing. Feel the power of this state to hold another person, another system in care and compassion.

Visualize the many ways you can actively use this state to shape the world. Maybe you are holding a loved one in your stream of ventral vagal energy to ease their suffering. Or perhaps you are the person with an enlivened ventral vagal system in the midst of dysregulation.

Take a moment to recognize the people in your life and the places in your world that are in need of your ventral vagal presence. Imagine moving into those connections from your state of ventral vagal abundance. Through the active, ongoing, intentional offering of ventral vagal energy, you are a beacon of kindness, generosity, goodness, compassion, friendship, and common humanity. Create an intention to beam benevolence.

A POLYVAGAL INSPIRED LIFE

▪ LIFE ON THE LADDER ▪

I began writing this piece while watching the snow fall in my backyard and finished it far away from home looking out at the sea. My nervous system is nourished by the storms that bring snow and by the sound of the sea, and it was in these two very different places that I settled in to write about what happens when we look at life through the lens of Polyvagal Theory.

I'm a licensed clinical social worker and love both the art and the science of psychotherapy. I have always believed therapists should have a basic understanding of how the brain works since we are engaging our clients in a process that is, in large part, meant to shape their brains in new ways. One of my most memorable experiences was the opportunity to visit a histology lab and work with a human brain. Holding a brain, finding the architectural landmarks, and watching a brain being sectioned gave me immense respect for the way we humans are created and the ways therapy can impact our neurobiology. My study of neurobiology gave me a framework to bring science into my work. Polyvagal Theory added the missing piece of the puzzle, giving me a new understanding of the ways in which our brains and bodies are inextricably connected. This discovery has fueled my passion for training therapists and for teaching everyday people about the science of connection—what I call the science of feeling safe enough to fall in love with life and take the risks of living.

Connection is at the heart of well-being and is a cornerstone of Polyvagal Theory. We have a natural drive toward connection, and I believe our biology inherently knows how to support this. Our nervous systems know the way home to the state of ventral safety and from that place, connection is possible. The pathways home are already there waiting for us. They may be obscured or unfamiliar and we may not have traveled them recently. However, as we find our way to a ventral state for just a micro-moment—when we experience a glimmer—we are reminded our nervous systems know the way.

We have a built-in longing to be connected to self, to others, to the world, and to Spirit. When we are pulled out of connection into protection, we suffer physically and psychologically. If we look at illness and wellness through the lens of the activation of autonomic states, illness can be thought of as the outcome of a nervous system that is dysregulated in a specific way, while wellness is a quality of a nervous system that is guided by the ventral vagal system. When the regulating energy of the ventral vagal system is unavailable or unpredictably available, dysregulation brings suffering. Without a critical mass of ventral energy in the system, disintegration, dysregulation, and distress are the result.

With an anchor in ventral, what would otherwise take us into a survival state of sympathetic mobilization with fight and flight or dorsal collapse and shut down, is instead an experience of safety and connection. The sympathetic and dorsal vagal systems work in the background doing their everyday, nonreactive jobs: sympathetic influencing heart and breath rhythms and bringing energy to fuel our system and dorsal managing our digestive processes. We have access to the energy of the sympathetic system and the quiet of the dorsal vagal state. We can be with reactive sympathetic or dorsal experiences and not be hijacked by them. Ventral vagal energy is the active ingredient that allows us to listen to the survival stories carried in our dysregulated states with curiosity and compassion. From an anchor in a ventral state, we can be informed by our stories and begin to create a coherent narrative—a life story that weaves all the pieces of our experience together.

In reality, none of us are continuously anchored in ventral, nor do I think that is an attainable or even desirable goal. We naturally move in and out of regulation in large and small ways throughout the day. There are times when the adaptive survival response of sympathetic mobilization or dorsal disappearing is needed. With the many moving pieces of people and connections that make up our lives, there is often a chaotic mix of autonomic energies. Over the course of a day, we travel down and up the hierarchy frequently. It's not the experience of being pulled out of ventral regulation that is the problem; it's being pulled out and getting stuck in a survival state. Being pulled into a sympathetic or dorsal response and not being able to return to the safety of a ventral state brings physical disease and emotional distress. The ability to flexibly move between states brings well-being. A flexible system is a resilient system . . . and a resilient system brings stories of possibility.

Our capacity to anchor in ventral and return from a moment of dysregulation is a process that is always being shaped. When we take the implicit experiences of the nervous system and bring them into explicit awareness, we move out of habitual response patterns into the possibility of change. To do this, we follow five "R's"—recognize, respect, regulate, reshape, re-story. Awareness allows us to recognize the autonomic state and accurately name it. We then respect the ways the state has activated in service of survival remembering that the nervous system is always acting to keep us safe. Putting the word "adaptive" before the words "survival response" reminds us that no matter how irrational our behavior in the moment may seem or how crazy our story may feel, a familiar cue of danger has come to life and our nervous system has enacted an old pattern of protection. Next, we bring a bit of ventral regulation and then begin to explore ways to reshape the pattern. Finally, we listen to the new story that is emerging. Through understanding how the autonomic nervous system takes in embodied, environmental, and relational experiences, we become active operators of our systems and authors of our own autonomic stories.

Understanding how to find the way back to a ventral state is key to living a balanced life. When we begin to find a foothold in regulation, we can look at any problem with the emergent properties that accompany a ventral state—curiosity, creativity, and the ability to see options and explore possibilities. From this place, we have the autonomic resources to see our experience in a new way, and we often find a path to resolution in a way we never thought possible.

A polyvagal perspective on life is not only a theory but a way of being in the world that is experienced from the inside out. Looking through the lens of the nervous system and listening to our autonomic stories, we shape our systems toward ventral regulation, and engage with our systems in new ways. When daily life is lived from a polyvagal perspective, we make a commitment to being aware of our autonomic experiences and becoming a regulated and regulating presence not only for ourselves but also for our partners, family members, friends, colleagues, and the people we naturally come into connection with during a day.

When we are firmly anchored in the ventral state, we feel truly embodied, present, safe, and ready to engage. Our brain adds information to help us engage with the world in an organized and resourceful way. We can be a witness to other people's stories and feel witnessed when we share our own. When we move out of the energy of the ventral pathway, our biology shifts away from connection toward protection, and we lose the ability to connect with these qualities and experiences. Our work is to know where we are on an autonomic map and be able to find our way home to the ventral state—back to the state that brings well-being. The question we ask ourselves is, what do I need in this moment to climb the autonomic ladder to safety?

Learning to stop, tune in, and explore the message our nervous system has received and now wants us to know is an important skill helping us see the world differently and trust our autonomic wisdom. With regular practice, the system's capacity for flexibility is resourced. With a flexible nervous system, our story is one of possibility. From a ventral state, our story is one of abundance.

Life on the Ladder in Challenging Times

We are living in a time of uncertainty and unpredictability where cues of danger seem to be everywhere, and cues of safety are hard to find and hold onto. As soon as we lose our anchor in a ventral state, we move out of regulation and enter a story of survival. One story may emerge from sympathetic activation that mobilizes fight or flight and another from dorsal immobilization and hopelessness that brings shut down and collapse. Every survival story takes us out of the ability to be curious, compassionate, and explore pathways to change.

Three elements contribute to our autonomic experience of well-being: context, choice, and connection. These elements help the nervous system anchor in safety and regulation. When they are present, we more easily find our way to regulation; when any one is missing, we feel off balance and experience a sense of unease. Around the world, events are taking place that impact the nervous system. The global disruption to context, choice, and connection significantly affects our capacity for regulation and relationship.

Humans are storytelling beings. Context helps us understand and make sense of an experience and sets the stage for our stories. Context comes from the Latin word *contexere*, meaning to weave together. Through the lens of the nervous system, context involves gathering information about how, what, and why in order to understand, and respond to, experiences. We live in a world of social media and fast-paced news feeds. We have access to a stream of information that is updated minute by minute and changes quickly. For some people, keeping up with unfolding events feels regulating and for others, it feels overwhelming. We each need to find our place on the continuum of awareness to overload.

With the proliferation of misinformation, we need to be savvy consumers and choose reliable sources of information. Context offers a frame for our understanding. When we lose faith in the accuracy of information, we can easily be pulled out of regulation into a pattern of protection.

Having choice is an autonomic signal of safety and extends an invitation to engage. More specifically, we know that both a lack of options and too many options send a warning while the number of choices that is just right in the moment enlivens our ventral vagal system. Sometimes fewer choices mean fewer decisions. This brings a sense of ease and the relief of being away from the overwhelming demands of daily life. Other times, less choice feels restrictive, activating a sympathetically driven state leading to a sense of desperation and the need to take action. In other situations, lack of choice brings feelings of despair and loss of agency, initiating a dorsal collapse and withdrawal from the world into isolation. Having unlimited choices can also be overwhelming as we feel lost in a sea of choices. It brings the same survival responses as not enough choice. There is no standard answer for the right number of choices. The presence and absence of choices can bring regulation, activation, or immobilization. As we navigate the day, we are more able to stay anchored in safety and regulation when the number of choices feels right for us in the moment. It is only from a ventral state that we can explore options with the support of our thinking brain and make a choice for ourselves and with others from the safety of a state of regulation.

Finally, we look at connection. We are wired to live in connection. With all the traumatic events taking place in the world, now more often than ever, being with other people brings a cue of danger instead of the possibility of safety and regulation. When opportunities for connection are missing, we carry the distress in our nervous system. We lose our sense of belonging and feeling safely tethered in the world. Our loneliness brings us pain. Our survival strategies come alive when we are feeling alone and out of attunement. We may reach out in desperation before retreating into despair. Without the regulating influence of the ventral vagus, we are driven to withdrawal and disconnection from partners, family, and friends. Unchecked, these actions become habitual response patterns.

The Path Forward

In these challenging times, when the world is in a "through the looking glass" moment, our challenge is to create a shared state of safety and a story of connection. Around the world, people are being displaced from their homes, work environments, and communities; are being disconnected from their support networks; and are feeling anxious and unsafe as they move through the world. This unprecedented disruption to the flow of life forces us to find new ways to be on our own and connect with others. Circumstances require that we learn how to safely turn inward and find nourishment in solitude and create new ways to reach out and come into connection.

Through the lens of the nervous system, the question is: How is our biology responding to what is happening in the world? As we look to answer that question, we see groups of people who are activated in the sympathetic survival energy of fight and flight and other groups who have been pulled into dorsal despair. Both groups are experiencing cues of danger that far outweigh any cues of safety and the safety/danger equation is tipped away from connection toward protection. They are held captive to the stories their brains create to make sense of the survival energy that is flooding their bodies. In order to engage in difficult conversations and work to create change, we need groups of people anchored in a ventral state whose brains are creating a story of possibility and who can begin to shift the balance toward safety in connection. In a ventral state, the ability to reflect and respond is strengthened. From an anchor in safety, we can shape both our own nervous systems and larger societal systems. The pathways we create out of necessity now can continue to support our individual and communal well-being in the future. Ventral vagal energy is the essential ingredient. From a ventral state, we can know our own experience, look at the autonomic experience of another person, appreciate the differences, and come into connection. We can find a way forward both as individuals and as a global community.

We are responsible for the autonomic information we are putting out into the world. Through neuroception and our social engagement systems, we are connected nervous system to nervous system. My autonomic state is broadcasting a welcome or a warning as I move through my day and every nervous system around me is receiving that message. When I feel overwhelmed by the state of the world, when change feels hopeless and my thoughts turn toward giving up, I remember I am communicating with the nervous systems around me and find my way home to ventral. The scientific definition of contagious is something that is transmitted by either direct or indirect contact. Ventral vagal energy is contagious. It has the potential to create a powerful ripple effect. By sending an autonomic message of safety and an invitation for connection, we can change the world one nervous system at a time.

ABOUT THE AUTHOR

DEB DANA, LCSW, is a clinician, consultant, and author who lectures internationally on how Polyvagal Theory informs work with trauma survivors. Deb's work shows how Polyvagal Theory applies to relationships, mental health, and trauma, and how we can use the organizing principles of Polyvagal Theory to change the way we navigate our daily lives.

Deb is well known for translating Polyvagal Theory into a language and an application that are both understandable and accessible—for clinicians and curious people alike. She is the author of *Polyvagal Exercises for Safety and Connection* and *Polyvagal Theory in Therapy*, as well as the *Polyvagal Card Deck* and *Polyvagal Flip Chart*, all available from W. W. Norton & Company, Inc.